Shape-Centered Representations: From Features to Applications

Dissertation
der Fakultät für Informations- und Kognitionswissenschaften
der Eberhard Karls Universität Tübingen
zur Erlangung des Grades eines
Doktors der Naturwissenschaften
(Dr. rer. nat.)

vorgelegt von
David Engel
aus Erbach

Tübingen
2010

Bibliografische Information der Deutschen Nationalbibliothek

Die Deutsche Nationalbibliothek verzeichnet diese Publikation in der
Deutschen Nationalbibliografie; detaillierte bibliografische Daten sind
im Internet über http://dnb.d-nb.de abrufbar.

ISBN 978-3-8325-2820-1

Logos Verlag Berlin GmbH
Comeniushof, Gubener Str. 47,
10243 Berlin
Tel.: +49 (0)30 42 85 10 90
Fax: +49 (0)30 42 85 10 92
INTERNET: http://www.logos-verlag.de

Tag der mündlichen Qualifikation: 09.02.2011
Dekan: Prof. Dr. Oliver Kohlbacher
1. Berichterstatter: Prof. Dr. Wolfgang Straßer
2. Berichterstatter: Prof. Dr. Heinrich H. Bülthoff

Ich erkläre hiermit, dass ich die zur Promotion eingereichte Arbeit mit dem Titel: 'Shape-Centered Representations: From Features to Applications' selbständig verfasst, nur die angegebenen Quellen und Hilfsmittel benutzt und wörtlich oder inhaltlich übernommene Stellen als solche gekennzeichnet habe. Ich versichere an Eides statt, dass diese Angaben wahr sind und dass ich nichts verschwiegen habe. Mir ist bekannt, dass die falsche Abgabe einer Versicherung an Eides statt mit Freiheitsstrafe bis zu drei Jahren oder mit Geldstrafe bestraft wird.

David Engel

Contents

Summary

Computer vision aims to teach machines and algorithms to 'see' with the ultimate goal of creating 'intelligent' applications and devices that can provide assistance to humans in a wide array of scenarios. This thesis presents an investigation of computer vision on three layers: low-level features, mid-level representations and high-level applications. Each of the layers depends on the previous ones while also generating constraints and requirements for them. At the application layer human-machine interfaces come into play and link the human perception to computer vision. By studying all layers we can gain a much deeper insight into the interplay of different methods, than by examining an isolated problem. Furthermore, we are able to factor constraints imposed by different layers and the users into the design of the algorithms, instead of optimizing a single method based purely on algorithmic performance measures.

After a brief introduction in Chapter 1, Chapter 2 addresses the feature layer and describes our novel shape-centered interest points that play a vital role throughout this thesis. These interest points are formed at location of high local symmetry as opposed to corner interest points which occur along the outline of shapes.

Experiments show that they are very robust with respect to common natural image transformations, such as scaling, rotation and the introduction of noise and clutter.

Based on these features Chapter 3 presents two strategies to build robust mid-level image representations. First, a novel feature grouping method is introduced. The scheme offers a powerful way to combine the advantages of shape-centered interest points, namely robustness and a tight connection to a unique shape, and corner-based interest points, namely strong descriptors. Furthermore, Chapter 3 introduces a novel set of medial feature superpixels, that represent a feed-forward way to divide the image into small, visually-homogeneous regions offering a compact and efficient mid-level representation of the image information.

Finally, Chapter 4 bridges the gap between computer vision and the human observer by introducing three applications that employ the shape-centered representations from the two previous Chapters. First, a multi-class scene labeling scheme is presented that produces dense annotations of images, combining a local prediction step with a global optimization scheme. Then, Section 4.2 introduces a novel image retrieval tool that operates on high-level semantic information. Such semantic annotations could be generated by automatic annotation schemes as the one described in the previous Section. Finally, the novel idea of predicting the detectability of a pedestrian in a driver assistance context is put forward and investigated.

The different modules of this thesis are tightly connected and inter-dependent, in the framework of shape-centered representations. The connections between the modules avails the possibility to feed information back from higher to lower layers and optimize the design choices there. This thesis provides a framework looking at static phenomena but the presented approach could be extended to the analysis of dynamic scenes as well.

Zusammenfassung

Maschinelles Sehen ist die Disziplin der Informatik, die versucht, Algorithmen und Maschinen 'Sehen' beizubringen. Das finale Ziel hierbei ist, 'intelligente' Applikationen und Geräte zu ermöglichen, die automatisiert für den Menschen relevante Aufgaben lösen. In dieser Dissertation werden drei Ebenen des maschinellen Sehens untersucht: einfache Bildmerkmale, zusammengesetzte Repräsentationen und Applikationen. Die einzelnen Ebenen basieren auf den Ergebnissen der darunterliegenden Ebene und definieren wiederum die Randbedingungen für diese. Auf der Applikations-Ebene wird durch die Schnittstelle zwischen Mensch und Maschine die Verbindung zwischen maschinellem Sehen und menschlicher Perzeption hergestellt. Die Untersuchung aller drei Ebenen erlaubt uns, eine tiefere Einsicht in die Interaktionen zwischen den verschiedenen Teilen zu gewinnen als die Untersuchung einer einzelnen Methode. Des Weiteren erlaubt uns diese Herangehensweise, die Algorithmen gezielter auf die Anforderungen der höheren Ebenen, beziehungsweise der menschlichen Endnutzer anzupassen, statt sie nur anhand algorithmischer Leistungskriterien zu optimieren.

Nach einer kurzen Einleitung in Kapitel 1, diskutiert Kapitel 2 die unterste Ebene des maschinellen Sehens und stellt einen neuartigen Detektor für Bildmerkmale vor, der Referenzpunkt im Zentrum von Formen findet. Diese Referenzpunkte bilden sich an Punkten mit hoher Bildsymmetrie. Experimente zeigen, dass die Merkmale sehr robust gegenber Transformationen wie Skalierung, Rotation, Rauschen und Veränderungen des Hintergrundes sind.

Basierend auf diesen Merkmalen stellt Kapitel 3 zwei Methoden vor, um robuste Bildrepräsentationen von mittlerer Komplexität zu erzeugen. Zuerst wird eine neuartige Methode zur Kombination von Bildmerkmalen vorgestellt. Der Algorithmus kombiniert die Vorteile von kantenbasierten Referenzpunkten (informationsreiche Kantenstruktur) mit den Vorteilen von formzentrierten Referenzpunkten (Stabilität gegen Rauschen und Hintergrundveränderung, sowie die eindeutige Zuordnung zu einer einzelnen Bildstruktur). Des Weiteren stellt Kapitel 3 einen neuen Algorithmus zum Erstellen von Superpixeln vor. Dieser Algorithmus zerteilt Bilder in homogene Regionen, die eine kompakte und effiziente Repräsentation der Bildinformation ermöglichen.

In Kapitel 4 wird die Applikations-Ebene betrachtet und die Verbindung zum menschlichen Betrachter hergestellt. Es werden drei Applikationen vorgestellt, die auf den formzentrierten Repräsentationen der vorangegangenen Kapitel basieren. Zuerst wird ein Algorithmus präsentiert, der semantische Annotationen für alle Pixel in einem Bild vorhersagt. Hierzu wird eine lokale Vorhersage der Objektkategorie mit einer globalen Optimierung kombiniert. Abschnitt 4.2 präsentiert eine neuartige Methode zur Bildersuche, die auf groben, semantische Informationen enthaltende, Zeichnungen, basiert. Abschließend präsentiere und untersuche ich die Idee, die Erkennbarkeit von Fußgängern in Bildern, im Kontext von Fahrassistenzsystemen, vorherzusagen.

Die einzelnen Teile der Arbeit basieren auf einander und sind in den Rahmen von formzentrierten Repräsentationen eingebettet. Die starken Verbindungen zwischen den Modulen ermöglicht es, das Design von zugrundeliegenenden Modulen an die Anforderungen von Applikationen oder menschlichen Nutzern anzupassen. Diese Arbeit beschäftigt sich mit statischen Situationen, aber die vorgestellten Methoden können, im Rahmen von zukünftiger Forschung, auch auf dynamische Szenen ausgeweitet werden.

Acknowledgments

First and foremost, I would like to thank Cristóbal Curio for his constant support and encouragement throughout my studies. This thesis would not have been possible without his creativity and readiness to help.

I am also very grateful to Prof. H.H. Bülthoff and Prof. W. Straßer for their friendly supervision and giving me the opportunity to work on an interesting topic in an outstanding, friendly and above all inspiring research environment.

This thesis would have been considerably harder in a different surrounding. Therefore, I would like to thank my friends and colleagues at the MPI for Biological Cybernetics, especially Nina for 1000 sent and received emails, Kathrin for fun times and the CoVi group, Björn and Christian, for great meetings. Also, I thank M. Breidt, M. Kleiner and B. Mohler for many fruitful discussions.

I would like to thank Liez and Nicki for making the good times even better and the hard times more bearable. I would also like to thank my friends from the lunch group, Chris, Eva, Mark, Sebi and Vroni, for all the great times we had, the projects we realized and the fishes we avoided.

Most of all, I would like to express my deepest gratitude to my family for everything they have done for me.

1

Introduction

*Much human ingenuity has gone into finding the ulti
mate 'Before'. The current state of knowledge can be
summarized thus: In the beginning, there was nothing,
which exploded.*

Terry Prachett - Lords and Ladies

Vision is one of the most impressive of human capabilities.
Based solely on the light waves that hit the retina after being
bounced of surfaces in the environment, it produces a vivid mental
representation of the outside world in our mind. The mental representation not only includes the position and orientation of surfaces
in the world but is enriched by knowledge about the objects in the
environment, their location and trajectories with respect to each
other and a multitude of other properties. This is by far no simple
task, since the environment is projected onto our retinas, yielding
an initial 2-D representation of the world comprised just of firing
rates of the rods and cones in our retina. Inferring the complex
and rich 3-D structure and the semantic relationships of objects in

Human vision is
an amazing ability
that creates a
vivid mental
representation of
the environment
from the retinal
image

1

it, based only on this very low-level representation is a very hard problem, to which a large part of the human cortex is devoted. This amazing feat has fascinated vision researchers for a long time (e.g. visual object categorization has been discussed by Aristotle in his treaties 'Categories' as early as 322 BC [4]).

Vision is investigated on the levels of physiology, psychophysics and computational analysis

Tremendous efforts have been undertaken to understand how vision, and human vision in particular, works on the levels of physiology, psychophysics and computational analysis. The algorithmic and computational analysis of vision tries to build models that operate on visual input data and reproduce the performance of parts of the human vision system in a computer and has sparked the field of computer vision research.

1.1 Computer Vision

Computer vision tries to build algorithms and machines that can 'see'

Computer vision is the discipline of algorithms and machines that 'see'. This algorithmic analysis of image data to extract high-level information is closely related to pattern recognition, image processing and machine learning. It furthermore shares problems with neurobiology and robotics and these interdisciplinary cooperations have proven useful for all fields.

The ultimate goal is to produce algorithms and devices that are useful to humans

One of the main goals of computer vision is to produce algorithms and methods that can solve vision problems automatically. Such algorithms can then be used by high-level applications that are useful for humans. One example would be computer vision algorithms that detect pedestrians in an image. This information could then be used by an autonomous vehicle or a driver assistance system to avoid dangerous situations and prevent accidents during driving. Another example is an object recognition algorithm that is able to detect and recognize different object categories in images, which in turn would allow image retrieval programs to help humans find specific images in a huge collection. Other areas

2

of application include biomedical scenarios (e.g. augmenting CT scan data during an operation), surveillance (e.g. automatic face detection at airports) and entertainment (e.g. human pose estimation for interactive games). Furthermore, computer vision can act as a method to advance the understanding of human vision. Computer vision can test models derived during psychophysical or neuro-anatomical studies and evaluate their performance in an algorithmic sense.

Since, even small images contain a large amount of data, focused studies in the field emerged as recently as the late 1970s, when the processing power of computers had increased sufficiently to deal with vision tasks. At first, vision was thought to be an easy problem, which would be quickly and easily implemented in machines. This turned out to be a misconception brought about by the ease with which humans can analyze and use visual input to solve complex tasks. Simplified problems such as detection and recognition of segmented shapes were solved easily but the performance seldom transfered to more natural settings including variability in pose, lighting and background. In such complex situations a high level of robustness is needed. Although computer vision has made considerable progress over the last decades, it still has a long way to go to achieve human level performance on most vision tasks (apart from above mentioned specialized contexts, such as industrial robotics, which can be very efficient but only in very constrained environments). This difference in performance between man and machine, even on basic vision tasks, is currently the main criterion to automatically discern between humans and machines in the Internet. For example, automatically deciding if an entry in an internet forum has been posted by human or by a computer script (i.e. advertisement) is the reverse problem of a Turing test: An algorithm has to decide if his counterpart is a human or a machine. Captchas [155] (the acronym for

The difficulty of algorithmic vision was initially underestimated because visual tasks are solved effortlessly by humans

The difficulty of some vision tasks is used for reverse Turing testing

3

Figure 1.1. Examples of Captchas exploiting the difficulties computer vision systems have at reading warped and corrupted text (top row) and at object detection and segmentation (bottom row). Images taken from http://www.captcha.net/

'Completely Automated Public Turing test to tell Computers and Humans Apart') are vision tasks that can be easily solved by humans, yet they still pose an extremely hard challenge to computer vision systems (see Figure 1.1).

Vision has to be viewed as an information theoretic problem and has to be analyzed on multiple levels

The advent of modern computer vision was triggered in the early 1980s by David Marr [98] and others who treated vision as an information theoretical problem and started to analyze it formally at three levels, paying special attention to the connections to human vision at the levels of ecological behavior and neurobiology:

- **The computational level:** What are the problems the system solves and why does it solve these problems? On this level, the visual system and its main functions are described. This level also provides the link between computer vision and ecologically relevant problems by requiring the researchers to specify the problem that is being addressed.

- **The algorithmic level:** How is the data processed and more specifically how is the visual data represented, stored and manipulated? On this level, the representations of the input and the output and the necessary transformations be-

4

tween them are made explicit. The computational analysis of vision happens here.

- **The implementation level:** How are these processes realized physiologically? What are the neural correlates of the algorithms? Here, the link from algorithmic description to neurobiology is made.

The emphasis on representations is an important notion in computer vision. Image encoding using features is a corner stone of all modern computer vision systems. This encoding scheme allows researchers to build robust systems that can deal with difficult natural images, as opposed to specialized systems that forgo more abstract representations for higher efficiency (but can only operate in constrained environments e.g. industrial sorting robots). Based on these representations, models can be formulated that allow vision algorithms to process visual information and perform high-level tasks such as object recognition or tracking.

Representation of information is crucial to build robust vision systems

In this thesis we are mostly focused on the algorithmic level of computer vision but also address the computational level in Chapter 4, where applications are introduced that link computer vision to a human observer. Most computer vision frameworks can be seen as being comprised of three layers:

Computer vision frameworks can be seen as consisting of three layers

- **Feature layer:** Extraction of low-level features in a feedforward manner. What features are used in this layer depends largely on the requirements imposed by the other layers but using biologically-inspired feature extraction methods has proven to be a valid option and presents a link to Marr's implementation level.

- **Combination layer:** Most computer vision frameworks do not build their representations directly on the information contained in the low-level features but combine information obtained at the first level to build a mid-level representation of the image data that is more robust against operations such as scaling, rotation, and the introduction of noise and clutter.

- **Application layer:** The final layer uses the information from the previous stages to solve a concrete problem such as object recognition, detection or tracking. Here machine learning techniques often play an essential role. The problems that are solved on this layer should be inspired by the questions arising from Marr's computational level. [98].

At the application layer the connection to the human observer is made

We look at all three layers and propose novel ways to address the problems arising on them, thus building a link between the low-level features, over the mid-level representations to the application layer. This allows us to link the algorithmic analysis of image data to the human observer for whom it should ultimately be beneficial. Having the human in-the-loop allows us to evaluate the performance at the different layers not only in an algorithmic but also in a psychophysical way (i.e. with human perception experiments). A core theme throughout our framework is the use of shape-centered representations, as they offer a versatile way to encode image information, which can be used in a generic way on all levels.

1.2 A Multi-Level Approach to Computer Vision

A crucial part of any computational vision pipeline is a robust representation. As opposed to most modern computer vision architectures, focusing on features extracted along edges of shapes, we exploit the observation that a shape-centered representation can yield a better robustness and moreover act as an integration device that combines information obtained at the edges in the image. Figure 1.2 outlines the main parts of this thesis along the three layers and the structure of the following chapters.

Shape-centered representations allow a high level of robustness and can integrate information from their surroundings

First, the feature layer is addressed. Chapter 2 introduces our novel shape-centered interest points that form the cornerstone of this thesis. These interest points occur at the center of shapes in the image as opposed to corner interest points which occur along the outlines of shapes. They are calculated as local maxima of symmetry detectors applied to vector flow fields. As experiments show, they are robust against many distortions that occur in natural images such as noise, clutter, scaling and rotation.

Chapter 2 introduces the low-level feature layer and our novel shape-centered interest points

Based on these features, Chapter 3 presents two novel ways for combining low-level features to obtain more powerful mid-level representations. Specifically, a novel mid-level representation is introduced in Section 3.1. Here, the shape-centered features are used to group together corner-based interest points. This scheme offers a powerful way to combine the advantages of shape-centered interest points (namely robustness against noise and clutter and their tight connection with a single shape) and corner interest points (namely strong descriptors of the local image structure) into a compact mid-level representation. Furthermore, medial-feature superpixels, a second way to obtain a powerful mid-level representation, are introduced in Section 3.2. They represent a feed-forward method to divide the image into a set of small visually-homogeneous segments

Chapter 3 presents two strategies to build robust mid-level representations of the local image structure

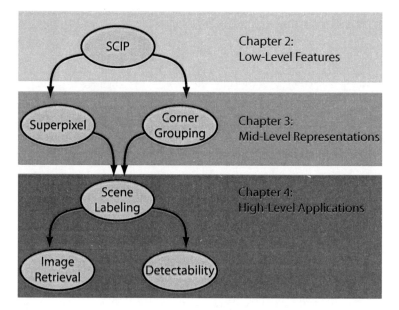

Figure 1.2. The overall flow of this thesis. Chapter 2 presents low-level shape-centered interest points (SCIP). Chapter 3 introduces our medial-feature superpixels and the grouping scheme that combine information from corner interest points to obtain strong mid-level representations. Chapter 4 details our application layer and presents algorithms based on the mid-level representations to do scene labeling, image retrieval and estimate the detectability of pedestrians in images. The arrows indicate the dependencies between the different parts of the framework.

(called superpixels) that offer a more compact and efficient way to represent the image information.

On the top-layer of our framework, Chapter 4 then demonstrates how these shape-centered representations can be employed in human-centered applications. First, a method to densely label scenes is presented in Section 4.1. This method produces dense multi-class labels for all pixels in an image, by combining a local classification stage with a global optimization scheme. Then, Section 4.2 presents a novel image retrieval scheme operating on semantic sketches made possible by such a scene labeling. The mid-level representations and features are also used in a human-machine interface in Section 4.3. Specifically, we estimate and optimize the detectability of pedestrians in a driver assistance context. Finally, Chapter 5 presents conclusions and an outlook.

Chapter 4 presents applications: a multi-class scene labeling framework, a novel image retrieval scheme and a novel method that predicts the detectability of pedestrians

2

Medial Features and Shape Centered Interest Points

Symmetry is what we see at a glance.

Blaise Pascal

This chapter presents a framework for extracting Shape Centered Interest Points (SCIP) from images. Section 2.1 reviews previous work in the field and describes the state-of-the-art. Next, Section 2.2 details how to obtain medial features, which are an image representation of intermediate complexity that encode the level of local symmetry for each point in the image. These medial features are an integral part not only of this chapter but also form the central building block of the methods and applications introduced in the following chapters. Section 2.3 explains how we can use the medial features to obtain scale and rotation-invariant shape-centered interest points that will be used by ensuing computer vision methods. Finally, Sections 2.4 highlights the properties of the shape-centered interest points such as robustness against

Shape-Centered Interest Points are a central building block of this and the following chapters

11

clutter and noise, their applicability for object detection, and their usefulness for image encoding.

2.1 State of the Art

Encoding images via interest points is a vital part of most modern computer vision systems

Image encoding has been recognized as a vital step for any computer vision algorithm [98]. Since pixels are just an artifact of image quantization, they are usually not informative by themselves. As a consequence, encoding an image purely by its color values is not useful for most tasks, thus calling for more compact and enriched image representations. It is common practice in computer vision to represent the information contained in an image using interest points. Interest points are locations in the image that are formed where the local image structure has special properties. For most computer vision tasks it is important to have interest points that are as robust as possible against common natural image transformation such as rotation, scaling and introduction of noise and/or background clutter. Running computer vision algorithms on a set of interest points derived from an image is a widespread method that is very reasonable since it e.g. yields substantial speedups and can help to suppress uninformative image content. The rationale behind this approach is that, since well chosen interest points are located at all informative image locations for the task at hand, the output of the algorithms will be the same whether it is computed densely on the whole image or only sparsely at interest points. Depending on their nature, interest points can be located along the outline of shapes or they can be located at the center of the shape or object of interest. Edge-based interest points are often called corner points and have proved to be very useful for many computer vision tasks as they can provide a highly informative description of local image properties. Several corner interest point detectors have been proposed

12

Figure 2.1. Examples of corner interest points (SIFT) (middle) and shape-centered interest points (right). Original image taken from [144].

such as the Moravec operator [108], the Scale-Invariant Feature Transform (SIFT) [91, 92] and interest points based on normalization around Harris [104, 135, 136] and Hessian [104] points. Other detectors from this category include edge-based region detectors [150] and intensity extrema detectors [151].

For segmented images, corner interest points offer a very powerful way for shape encoding. More natural images that contain background clutter on the other hand pose a harder problem (this will be discussed in detail in Section 2.3.1). Corner interest points are located directly on or at least close to the border between two shapes, thus it is likely that their associated descriptors contain information about the shape of interest as well as about background clutter. Differentiating between foreground and background is a hard and often ambiguous task.

Corner interest points are often located between several shapes

A class of interest points that is less prone to this problem are shape-centered interest points, often also called medial features. They occur at image locations where the local image structure or local shape is highly symmetrical. As they are located inside a shape, they are less likely to be disturbed if the background outside of the target shape changes. Such medial features of intermediate complexity have been recognized as being useful entities for both human object recognition [31, 74, 80, 148] and in computer vi-

Shape-centered interest points provide robustness against clutter

13

sion systems [115, 119]. Medial features share several similarities with blob detectors that aim at finding image locations or regions that are brighter or darker than their surroundings. It has been demonstrated that humans focus their gaze at locations of blob like structures during free visual search, indicating a high information content of features at shape-centered locations [73]. Most noticeable among the blob detectors are the Hessian of Gaussian (used e.g. by Bay et al. [7]) and the Difference of Gaussians (DoG), which was prominently proposed by Marr [99]. Blob detection can also refer to region detectors such as the MSER [101] and PCBR [35].

Medial features based on GVF fields are very robust against noise

As a more general concept, the strength of medial features in vision has been emphasized by Kimia and others, e.g. [141, 36]. In this line of research, wave propagation models based on the solution of the Eikonal equation in the image plane have been employed to derive features for shape matching tasks. Alternatively, gradient vector flow (GVF) fields [162] have been recognized for the computation of medial features. The GVF approach made many vision tasks amenable for cluttered environments. Initially developed for long range contour alignment, GVF has recently been investigated for shape characterization of segmented silhouettes [55, 56], as well as for scale-invariant object recognition in clutter, based on learned patch codebooks (see Section 2.4.1 and Engel et al. [41]). Lu et al. proposed the M-Rep model [93] that has been successfully applied to 3D shape analysis and registration. This approach particularly learns the statistics of so-called medial atoms, which are used for similarity judgments of graph model structures.

2.2 Constructing Medial Features

Local symmetry measures how 'shape-centered' a point is

The goal of medial features is to provide a measure of local symmetry. This means that we are looking for a function f that takes an

14

edge map E of an image as input and yields for every pixel a scalar representing the amount of its shape-centeredness or symmetry.

$$f(E, x, y) = \text{level of local symmetry at } (x, y) \qquad (2.1)$$

There are different forms of symmetry. A face for example is roughly symmetric with respect to the median sagittal plane and a ball is point symmetrical with respect to its center. More complex definitions allow to describe e.g. the helical symmetry of a screw. Detecting such high-level symmetries can be quite difficult and would be neither plausible nor desirable to be used in our feed-forward feature framework. Based on these considerations, we define symmetric points as locations where the closest edges in different directions are equally far apart. This very basic definition has the benefit of being extensible beyond finding points or lines that correspond to point- or plane-symmetries. We are able to evaluate Equation 2.1 densely at each image location availing the option of calculating a measure of symmetry at each pixel. Locations with high local symmetry are points where many of the closest edges are equidistant while locations with a low local symmetry have only few equidistant edges in their vicinity. An illustration of this can be seen in Figure 2.2.

Local symmetry can be evaluated at every position in an image

The classical way to calculate the local symmetry is based on the distance transformation D_T (e.g. [3, 16]):

$$D_T(E, P) = \inf_{e' \in E} |P, e'| \qquad (2.2)$$

where $P \in \mathbb{R}^2$ is the image location where we want to evaluate D_T and e' are the locations where the edge detector found edges in the image. The distance transformation $D_T(E, P)$ (we abbreviate $D_T(E, P)$ with $D_T(E)$ from here on) of a binary edge map E assigns to each image location the distance to the nearest edge in pixel (an example is depicted in Figure 2.3). There exist very effi-

D_T yields the minimal distance to the closest edge for each pixel

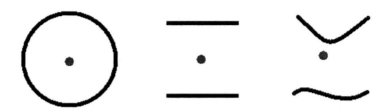

Figure 2.2. Different levels of local symmetry. Edges are illustrated in black and the point where we evaluate the local symmetry is shown in red. **Left:** In the center of a circle all locally relevant edges are equidistant leading to a very high local symmetry. **Middle:** Along a ridge we have significantly lower local symmetry. **Right:** At arbitrary points on an unspecific shape all edges have different distances and we have a very low and on the edges even negative local symmetry.

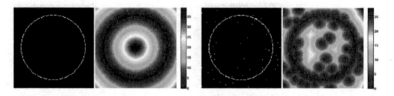

Figure 2.3. Example of pairs of edge maps E and their associated distance transformations $D_T(E)$. The left pair shows a clean edge map of a circle and $D_T(E)$, which yields the distance to the nearest edge pixel (the color-maps indicate the distance in pixel). The two images on the left depict the instability of $D_T(E)$ against even small amounts of noise.

cient implementations to calculate $D_T(E)$. The peaks and ridges of this distance transformation are points of high local symmetry (as per Equation 2.1) because they are equidistant to at least two edges.

D_T is not stable against noise

A major drawback of calculating symmetry this way is the lack of robustness against noise. Even a single erroneously detected edge pixel can degrade whole areas of D_T as shown in Figure 2.3 (right). It follows that, either extensive preprocessing is required to achieve a very robust edge map E or a more robust way to find local symmetry is needed. To address this problem, Curio [31] proposed a novel way to calculate local symmetry using GVF fields, which will be extended in Section 2.2 ff. (see also Engel et al. [41]).

2.2.1 Gradient Vector Flow Fields

Gradient vector flow fields (GVF) were proposed by Xu et al. [162, 163] as an external force for large range contour deformation to detect even concave shape boundaries. It is calculated as the diffusion gradient of the edge map E of an image. Any kind of edge map can be used but continuous edge energies such as the squared sum of orthogonal Gabor filters usually offer good results as they allow a smoother approximation of the gradients in the image. The algorithm simulates a diffusion process in which E can be thought of as energy that is being distributed throughout the image resulting in the GVF field, which represents the directions of the energy flow at each pixel. Specifically, the GVF field is the vector field $V(x,y) = [u(x,y), v(x,y)]$ that minimizes the following energy function:

> $V(x,y)$ is the result of a simulated diffusion process

$$\epsilon = \int \int \underbrace{g\left(|\nabla E|\right) |V - \nabla E|^2}_{\text{data term}} + \underbrace{h\left(|\nabla E|\right) \nabla^2 V}_{\text{smoothing term}} \, dx dy \qquad (2.3)$$

This cost function is subject to the iterative optimization of V until convergence and is obtained using variational calculus. The data term guarantees stability of the vector field $V(P)$ at point $P = (x,y)$ near an edge in the edge map E, whereas the second term is responsible for the suppression of spurious edges and the propagation of orientation information across the image. The optimization aims to accomplish the two competing goals of preserving the orientation information at the gradients and creating a smooth flow field across the image. The functions g and h determine the

> The GVF creates a smooth field V that complies with the image gradients

17

trade off between these two conflicting goals. They are designed to be complementary, enforcing stricter adherence to the underlying edge map at locations of high gradient magnitude and smoothness where the magnitude is low. For our purposes, we followed the implementation of [163] using a constant for $h = 0.12$ and the magnitude of the edge map $g = |\nabla E|^2$ for data function.

The optimal edge operator is task-dependent

Equation 2.3 also shows the influence of the choice of the edge operator that creates E. Discrete edge detectors such as thresholded Sobel filters or Canny [21] yield very sharp and detailed edge maps that will produce a finer GVF field along the edges, but continuous edge detectors such as Gabor filters will allow a better approximation of the gradients in the image resulting in a smoother vector field. Which edge detector is best can therefore depend on the application at hand. Example results from two different edge detectors are shown in Figure 2.4.

We normalize the solution of $V(P)$ at each image location resulting in $V_N(P)$:

$$V_N(P) = \frac{V(P)}{\|V(P)\|} \tag{2.4}$$

Our assumption is that $V_N(P)$ closely approximates the gradient of the L_2-norm distance function $\nabla D_T(P)$:

$$\nabla D_T(P) \approx V_N(P) = V(P)/\|V(P)\| \ \forall P. \tag{2.5}$$

Singularities in V_N are locations of high local symmetry

This implies that instead of looking for local maxima of the distance transformation D_T we can now find points of high local symmetry by searching for locations where the vector field $V_N(P)$ collides. Pizer et al. [119] suggested a singularity detection framework based on the divergence of V_N which is called the flux flow:

$$\mathcal{F} = \frac{\int_{\delta R} \langle V, \mathcal{N} \rangle \, ds}{\int_{\delta R} ds}, \tag{2.6}$$

18

where $\mathcal{N}$ denotes the inward-pointing normals on a ring through which the flux flow $\mathcal{F}$ is computed. The computation of this ring integral at each point in the image can be implemented for the two components of V_N as two convolutions with two precomputed kernels containing the two normal vector components of that ring, respectively. The size of the ring along which the flux flow is computed contains a trade-off between smoothing (which implies suppression of noise) and loss of information. Larger diameters produce a more smooth and stable flux flow field while smaller diameters are able to capture finer details. A diameter of 7 pixels is a good trade-off between the two goals (smoothing and loss of information) for most situations. Several results for different ring diameters are shown in Figure 2.4. Using the Gabor filtering (top row) produces a smoother and stronger skeleton in the middle of the pedestrian while the Canny (lower row) edge operator is able to capture finer details.

$\mathcal{F}$ is the flux flow of the normalized vector field

Since, the computation of the GVF is an iterative process (the error in Equation 2.3 is optimized stepwise), we have to ensure that the solution is fully converged before computing the ring integral. Stopping before full convergence (see Figure 2.5) can lead to undesired local extrema of $\mathcal{F}$ that in turn can lead to erroneous shape-centered interest points. However, determining how many steps are needed until convergence is quite difficult. Checking for convergence during the optimization by calculating the differences in the vector fields between consecutive steps $\|V_n(P) - V_{n-1}(P)\| < \sigma$, where σ as a preset stop criterion, turned out to be impractical. Multi-scale approaches are better adapted to solving this problem. For real world applications that may contain such disadvantageous examples, images should be processed in the original resolution as well as $\frac{1}{2}$ and $\frac{1}{4}$ the size. If not stated otherwise we ran the GVF for 200 iterations, which ensures full convergence for all relevant situations we have encountered thus far.

$\mathcal{F}$ has to be computed on the fully converged vector field V_N

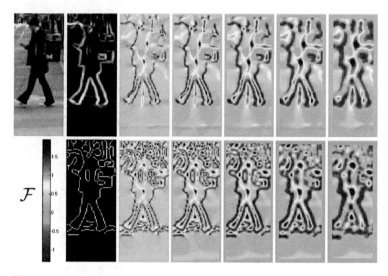

Figure 2.4. The influence of the radius of the ring for the ring integral computation and the edge operator on the flux flow $\mathcal{F}$. Top left shows the original image. The upper row was created using a continuous Gabor edge operator while the lower row is based on the Canny edge operator. The five flux flow fields $\mathcal{F}$ were computed using ring radii of 1,2,3,4 and 5, respectively. The scale shows the absolute value of the flux flow. Highly symmetrical areas have positive values while salient edges are assigned negative values.

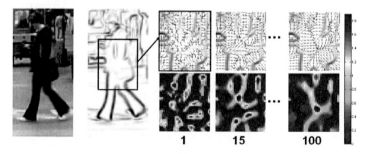

Figure 2.5. The iterative evolution of the GVF and the flux flow $\mathcal{F}$ over time (the shown flux flow has been clipped at 0). Numbers below the images indicate iteration cycle.

The resulting flux flow field $\mathcal{F}$ yields a scalar at each image location corresponding to the local symmetry. One direct way to utilize this information is to derive shape-centered interest points. The next Section will detail the algorithm for obtaining these interest points, their properties and the rationale for using them.

2.3 Properties of Shape-Centered Interest Points

This Section explains how we use the medial features, or more precisely the flux flow field $\mathcal{F}$, to derive shape-centered interest points (SCIP). The formed interest points can be roughly clustered into three groups (circular, end-stopping and ridges) that are characterized by the value of $\mathcal{F}$ at the center location. Furthermore, we detail how we estimate a local scale and orientation at the interest points making them invariant against rotation and scaling.

Shape-centered interest points (SCIP) can be derived from $\mathcal{F}$

To identify the interest points, we employ a non-maximum suppression scheme combined with thresholding. This thresholding guarantees that interest points are only formed at locations of high symmetry. The non-maximum suppression then detects local maxima from the thresholded $\mathcal{F}$ while ensuring that all interest points (IP) are at least d_{IP} pixels apart. This avoids too dense sampling along ridges, since every pixel on a ridge is per definition a local maximum, which would lead to a high amount of interest points there.

Non-maximum suppression to sample SCIPs from $\mathcal{F}$

Because of the normalization of the vector field, as described in Equation 2.4, the values of $\mathcal{F}$ do not depend on the magnitude of the gradients of the edge map E. This has the advantage of yielding flux flow values that are directly linked to the form of the enclosing shape and are thusly interpretable. There are three major classes of SCIPs that naturally emerge when clustering the surroundings of the interest points according to the values

There are three distinct classes of SCIPs

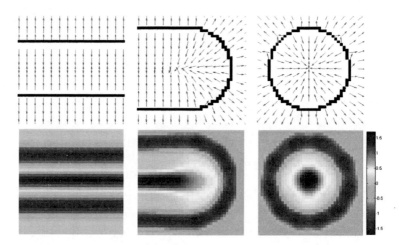

Figure 2.6. The three main classes of shape-centered interest points from left to right: ridge, end-stop and circular structure. Top row shows the normalized GVF field $\mathcal{V}_N$ superimposed on the corresponding edge maps and the lower row depicts the flux flow $\mathcal{F}$. We can note that $\mathcal{F}$ is strongly negative at the salient edges.

of $\mathcal{F}$: ridges, end-stop locations and circular shapes. Examples of these classes are shown in Figure 2.6. The values associated with the three different classes are approximately 1.3 for ridges, 1.6 at end-stopping points and 1.8 at locations with circular symmetry (for a normal ring radius of 5 pixels and a ring width of 3 pixels). On the salient edges in the image $\mathcal{F}$ will take negative values of up to -1.5, which we will exploit later in Section 2.3.2 to estimate the local scale at the interest points.

Interest point positions can shift slightly along ridges

Incorporating the distance constraint of d_{IP} pixels between the interest points leads to the problem that their positioning along the ridges is not fixed (e.g. sampling every fourth point along a ridge returns a different set of points depending on the starting conditions). This might seem like a drawback, but the instability occurs only along straight ridges. When choosing a d_{IP} of four

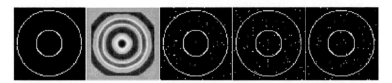

Figure 2.7. The positions of the SCIP wander in the presence of noise, while the interest point in the center stays fixed. This phenomenon only occurs in the presence of strong noise on the edge map (here 5% of all pixels were flipped).

pixels (which we did in our experiments), there is a maximal imprecision of two pixels between different computations on the same data, which should easily be coped with by the subsequent computer vision algorithms in the remainder of the thesis.

Another source of imprecise interest point positioning along the ridges stems from noise. The flux flow values along the ridges can be very similar, leading to situations where noise does not change the structure of $\mathcal{F}$ but influences the concrete values along the ridges enough to change the positions of the maxima as shown in Figure 2.7. But, as this phenomenon only appears in the presence of very strong noise and only applies to ridge structures, it is not a relevant problem. End-stop points and circular structures still generate the same unique interest points, which can also be seen in Figure 2.7. Furthermore, as the local shape along ridge-like structures is usually quite uniform one can presume that the exact position of the interest points influence the descriptors and the recognition rates only weakly. For example, when identifying a leg, the general 'tube'-structure and the positions of the end-stop interest points, and not the exact position of the center of the leg, are important.

Noise can influence the positioning of SCIPs along the ridges

23

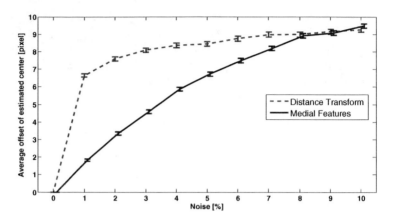

Figure 2.8. The robustness of our medial features and the distance transform against noise. The x-axis denotes which percentage of pixels on the edge map were randomly flipped before the GVF computation. The y-axis indicates the average offset of the estimated circle center from the true center of the circle. The true circle radius was 25. Medial features clearly outperform the distance transformation in this case. Error bars indicate standard error.

2.3.1 Robustness Against Noise and Clutter

SCIPs are more robust against noise than the maxima of D_T

Now, we will demonstrate that our shape-centered interest points possess a higher robustness against noise than the standard method of finding symmetry points that rely on detecting the local maxima of the distance transform D_T. The task we chose is the detection of the symmetry point in the center of a circle with radius 25 pixel (c.f. Figure 2.8). We start with an edge map of the circle and add increasing amounts of noise by randomly setting pixels in the edge map to one. The maximum of the flux flow field and the distance transform is presumed to be the best estimate for the center of the shape. Figure 2.8 plots the distance and standard deviation of the estimated center to the real center of the circle averaged over 500 trials for different levels of noise.

24

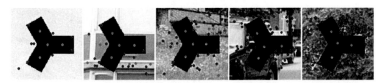

Figure 2.9. Examples depicting the superior robustness against different levels of clutter of SCIPs (blue) over corner interest points (here SIFTs in red). The positions of the red corner interest point is influenced much more by the clutter than the positions of the shape centered interest points.

As we can see, our medial features provide significantly higher robustness against noise than the symmetry point detection using the ridges on D_T. This is because they are based on an anisotropic diffusion process that suppresses spurious noise. It could be argued that a preprocessing step such as edge map erosion would increase the performance of the symmetry point detection based on the distance transform. However, this would also hold true for our medial feature based approach. Furthermore, we view the noisy input edge map as the result of such preprocessing steps, which may still not be able to produce a noise free image implying the need for our robust interest point detection scheme.

The GVF approach suppresses spurious noise

A common problem in computer vision is that interest points are often formed or influenced by intersections between the shape of interest and background clutter. Medial features are less sensitive to clutter than corner interest points (see examples in Figure 2.9). The vector field V_N on the inside of the tripod only depends on the edges of the tripod and the medial features are therefore not influenced by clutter. The SIFT interest points depend on local image structure close to the edges and consequently change positions as the background forms new corners with the shape of interest.

SCIPs are very robust against clutter

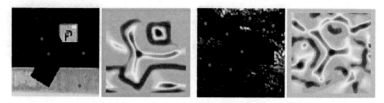

Figure 2.10. Failure cases of the robustness against clutter. Depicted are shape-centered interest points on tripod-like shapes embedded into clutter and the corresponding degenerated flux flow fields $\mathcal{F}$.

Degenerated edge
maps can lead to
erroneous interest
points

Shape-centered interest points are influenced by background clutter only when the clutter has a similar appearance as the shape of interest. In such a case no meaningful edges can be formed, the flux flow degenerates and the maxima of $\mathcal{F}$ and consequently the interest points are formed at incorrect positions. Figure 2.10 depicts such failure cases. These cases cannot be circumvented since the boundary information is missing and could only be 'hallucinated' by a top-down process that has further information about the shape it is dealing with (seeing a person dressed in black (e.g. a Ninja) in front of a black wall at night can be really difficult albeit the cost of missing the person can be quite high). Here we are only dealing with bottom-up interest point detection and can therefore neglect this problem.

2.3.2 Scale and Rotation Invariance

Interest points
should be
invariant against
scaling and
rotation

Objects in images can occur in a wide variety of scales and viewing angles. For computer vision tasks, such as recognition and classification, these changes are mostly irrelevant as we want to be able to detect objects equally well across all orientations and a wide range of scales. Consequently, a certain degree of invariance against scaling and rotation is a very desirable property of interest points. A common way to achieve such invariances is to estimate a local scale and orientation at each interest points. These local estimates allow the algorithm to describe the shape surrounding the interest point in a manner that is not influenced by scaling or rotation.

Estimating a local scale on edge-centered interest points (such as Harris-Corners [60] or SIFT [92]) is routinely done by maximizing some measure of local image properties on a pyramid of scales (c.f. [89, 159] for an analysis of automatic scale selection using the notion of scale space). Though the practical value of these scale estimates has proved to be useful in many applications it is theoretically and practically unsatisfying. Local scales can only be meaningful in association with surrounding shapes. Edges are by definition locations between two shapes and consequently the local scale estimation at edge-centered interest points can not be meaningful as it is associated with at least two shapes.

Local scales at corner interest points are mostly not meaningful

Shape-centered interest points such as the ones proposed here are tightly connected with the surrounding shape and provide an elegant and intuitive way to estimate a meaningful local scale. In the following paragraphs, we detail the two methods for estimating local scales at SCIP that we have proposed (Engel and Curio [41, 42]).

SCIPs allow us to estimate a meaningful local scale

The properties of the underlying GVF leads to interest points that are formed by at least two equidistant salient edges. Consequently, a local scale can be estimated by detecting the preserved image edges of the flux flow field $\mathcal{F}$ that led to the interest point. We do this by using a scanning process that computes the mean flux flow of continuously growing discs centered at the interest points. For reasons of simplicity we rewrite the flux flow $\mathcal{F}$ in polar coordinates:

A scanning process can find the edges that lead to the maxima in $\mathcal{F}$

$$\mathcal{F}(\alpha, r, x_0, y_0) = \mathcal{F}(x_0 + \sin(\alpha) * r, y_0 + \cos(\alpha) * r) \qquad (2.7)$$

27

where (x_0, y_0) is the position of the interest point in image coordinates, and α and r are the angle and radius of the point (x, y) relative to the interest point. We estimate the scale by computing the mean flux flow of discs centered at the interest points. Equation 2.8 shows the mapping $\mathcal{S}\,(r, x_0, y_0)$, which is derived from the flux flow field and maps from the radius of the disc r to the mean flux flow energy $\mathcal{S}$

$$\mathcal{S}\,(r, x_0, y_0) = \frac{\int_0^r \int_0^{2\pi} \mathcal{F}\,(\alpha, r, x_0, y_0)\, d\alpha dr}{\pi r^2} \qquad (2.8)$$

$\mathcal{S}(r)$ is the mean flux flow of disc around the interest point and will hit a minima at the local scale r'

$\mathcal{S}(r)$ measures the mean flux flow energy of a disc with radius r centered at an interest point. We compute $\mathcal{S}(r)$ by integrating over all directions α and all radii from 0 to r. Going back to the notion that the flux flow $\mathcal{F}$ is high at locations of high local symmetry and negative at the salient edges in the image we can see that $\mathcal{S}(r)$ will hit a minimum with respect to r just as it fully engulfs the edges leading to the formation of the interest point (see Figure 2.11). For smaller values of r, the disc will not include the strongly negative values of $\mathcal{F}$ at the edges. As r grows and the disc grows beyond the edges that led to the formation of the interest point, it will include points of $\mathcal{F}$ that lie outside the shape associated with the current interest point and have a positive sign. We can generally assume that there is either nothing on the outside the shape of interest (in case of segmented images) or only uncorrelated clutter. In both cases, the average flux flow outside the shape will be higher than on the relevant edges. The only case that violates this assumption is if the density of edges on the outside the shape is higher than the density of the edges that formed the interest point. But this is a very pathological case. We thusly conclude that we can find the edges that led to the formation of the interest point and the local scale r' by detecting the first local minimum of $\mathcal{S}$ as described in Equation 2.9.

28

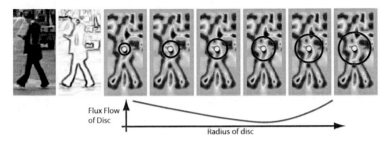

Figure 2.11. Estimating the local scale at an interest point. From left to right: An image and the edge map. A growing disc (black circle) around a shape-centered interest point (yellow dot) on the associated flux flow field $\mathcal{F}$. The mean flux flow $\mathcal{S}(r)$ on a disc with radius r is computed according to Equation 2.8. The graph below the Figure shows a depiction of the function $\mathcal{S}(r)$. The first minimum corresponds to the estimated local scale r'.

$$r' = \underset{r}{\arg\min}\left(r\,\middle|\,\mathcal{S}(r)\,\frac{d}{dr} = 0\right) \qquad (2.9)$$

A more intuitive explanation of the local scale estimation is depicted in Figure 2.11. One can picture the process of determining the local scale as the reverse process to the creation of the shape-centered interest points. During their formation, we simulate a diffusion process that aligns the GVF field according to the flow direction from the salient edges to the interest points. For scale estimation, we scan out from the interest points to the salient edges as determined by $\mathcal{F}$. This *filling in* step followed by a *scanning outwards* is similar to the idea of *filling in to find out* coined by Curio [31]. Scale estimation is the reverse process to the interest point formation

In the presence of high amounts of noise, the scale estimation can become unstable when following the approach described in Equation 2.8. To counteract this, we have proposed in [42] to accumulate the scalar product between the normalized GVF field and a disc containing an outward pointing vector field $O(\alpha, r) \in \mathbb{R}^2$ (written in polar coordinates). This approach has the advantage Higher robustness against noise can be achieved by using the direction of V_N

29

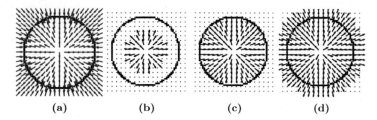

Figure 2.12. Estimating the local scale with $\mathcal{S}'$ (see Equation 2.10). We want to estimate the local scale at the center of a ring shaped edge map (in white) with the GVF field as shown in blue (a). We compute the sum of the pointwise scalar product with the three inward pointing vector fields $O(\alpha, r)$ (b)-(d). The first one (b) does not capture all correctly aligned GVF vectors. The second one (c) is just right. The third one (d)overshoots the correct local scale and consequently accumulates GVF vectors pointing in the wrong direction thus leading to a local maximum of $\mathcal{S}'(r)$ at the correct disc size.

of accumulating only the part of the shape that is actively contributing to the interest point while penalizing the area outside the shape where the GVF vectors point in opposite directions and therefore add a negative value to the sum.

$$\mathcal{S}'(r, x_0, y_0) = \frac{\int_0^r \int_0^{2\pi} < \mathcal{V}_N(\alpha, r), O(\alpha, r) > d\alpha dr}{\pi r^2} \qquad (2.10)$$

Substituting $\mathcal{S}$ with $\mathcal{S}'$ does not influence the search for the local scale es described in Equation 2.9. We still scan through all scales and take the first minimum of r' as the local scale the current interest point. Figure 2.12 shows a depiction of the computation of $\mathcal{S}'$.

Efficient implementation by using a lookup-table and cumulative summation

A linear scan through all scales would be slow and inefficient. We have implemented this process efficiently by first sorting all relevant pixels of $\mathcal{F}$ according to their distance from the interest points. On the resulting vector we calculate the cumulative sum. The value of $\mathcal{S}(r)$ for a given r is then the cumulative sum at the

30

last pixel with distance smaller or equal to r divided by the number of pixels on the disc. The sorting step can be precomputed as a static reordering of a vector using a lookup table while building the cumulative sum and the divisions can be calculated very efficiently.

This formulation allows us to estimate stable and meaningful local scales for each interest point. To gain further invariance against larger changes of scaling, we can apply the whole detection pipeline on a pyramid of scaled images or edge maps. How the scaling factors between the different steps of the pyramid should be chosen depends on the robustness of the scale estimation and will be detailed along with an evaluation of the invariance properties in Section 2.4.

Applying the scale estimation on a pyramid of scaled images

We will now turn to the rotation invariance, which is another desirable property for interest points. Rotation invariance means that the same interest points can be found and identified at different viewing angles. Building on the previous scale estimation we can estimate an orientation at the interest point and use this direction to describe the appearance of the image vicinity of the interest point in a scale and rotation-invariant manner.

Local orientation estimation yields rotation-invariant interest points

We estimate a local orientation by extracting a disc with radius r' (the estimated local scale) from the flux flow field $\mathcal{F}$. We threshold the resulting patch at value one thus retaining only the ridges, end-stop locations and points with circular symmetry. We then take the coordinates of the pixels above the threshold relative to the interest point and calculate the eigenvectors of the autocorrelation matrix (a principle component analysis (PCA) c.f. [72, 117]). The eigenvector corresponding to the largest eigenvalue indicates the direction of the largest variance. We take this vector as the local orientation associated with the current interest point. Figure 2.13 shows examples of interest points, their associated local scales and the estimated local orientations.

The first principle component of the thresholded $\mathcal{F}$ corresponds to the local orientation

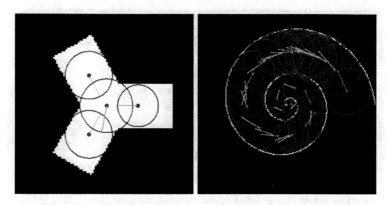

Figure 2.13. Examples of shape-centered interest points (red dots), local scale estimates (red circles) and estimated orientations (green lines). The interest points, local scales and orientations behave nicely and intuitively.

At circular or ridge structures the local orientations is ambiguous

At circular locations, the local orientation is undefined since the surrounding shape is identical for all rotations. This is reflected in our orientation estimation scheme. Both principle components will have very similar eigenvalues and all orthogonal directions of the eigenvectors are equally correct solutions. The estimated orientation for such circular shapes therefore depends on noise and is undefined (random). This is correct and should not reduce the recognition rate of the shape since all estimated orientations produce very similar appearances. A similar ambiguity occurs for interest points that are drawn along ridges. At these locations, $\mathcal{F}$ is mirror symmetric and consequently the direction of the first principle component is equally likely to point in a 180° rotate direction. The full pipeline that yields our interest points, the respective local scales and orientations is shown in Figure 2.14.

An efficient Matlab implementation is available

The feature extraction pipeline is currently implemented in Matlab and the GVF computation is capsulated in MEX/C++ code to improve the efficiency. The whole pipeline in its present form takes on average 2.2 seconds to run on a standard office

32

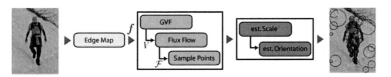

Figure 2.14. The SCIP extraction pipeline. First the edge map is calculated, then the normalized GVF is computed and interest points are sampled from the flux flow $\mathcal{F}$. At these SCIPs, the local scale and orientation is estimated.

Part of the pipeline	Average runtime [sec] for medium and large images	
Edge Map	0.09	0.53
GVF and Flux Flow	1.72	16.56
Sampling interest points	0.36	4.64
Scale estimation	0.02	1.23
Orientation estimation	0.01	0.29
Total	2.21	23.27

Table 2.1. Computation time for all steps in the pipeline for medium sized images [400 × 300] and large images [1600 × 1200].

desktop computer running Windows XP^{TM} for average sized images. For a more detailed compilation of the running times of the different parts of the pipeline and different image sizes confer to Table 2.1.

The current implementation is not yet optimized for speed. The iterative optimization of the GVF is well parallelizable and there are now GPU implementations available, which will significantly reduce the computation time (c.f. Kleiner et al. [77]).

2.4 Evaluation of Invariance Properties

The standard evaluation is designed for affine region detectors

In this Section, we present an evaluation of the invariance proper-ties of the medial features. For interest point operators that detect affine regions (oriented ellipses) a standard performance evaluation dataset provided by Mikolajczyk et al. [107, 105] exists. As medial features generate interest points that are located where maximal inscribing discs fit, our algorithm yields circular regions of interest. There is no straight-forward way to fit affine regions to the flux flow field at the interest points. As the test from [107] calculates the region overlap of two detected ellipses after an affine camera transformation, it is not applicable to our interest points.

Our scale estimation can compensate downscaling up to factor 0.5

We test the robustness of our features against scale changes with an experiment. We took images from the MIT StreetScenes Database [14], which will be discussed and used more thoroughly later in Chapter 4. It is a database containing photographies of ur-ban street scenes and is well suited for the task since it contains a wide array of local scales. We took 100 images from this database and computed our SCIP on them and estimated their local scales. To test the performance, we rescaled the images and reestimated the local scales at the interest points. The average difference be-tween the original and estimated scales are shown in Figure 2.15. The robustness of the scale estimation is encouraging and allows us to build strong object detectors based on these features. Still, for downscaling, the estimation error rises rather drastically around a scale factor of around 0.5. Consequently, when building a com-puter vision system that should be able to e.g. detect an object in a range beyond these scales one should extract the interest points on pyramid of scaled images. Based on our findings, we suggest downsampling the image by $\frac{1}{2}$ and $\frac{1}{4}$ to achieve a good coverage of all relevant scales at which objects can occur.

To provide further evidence for the robustness of the scale esti-

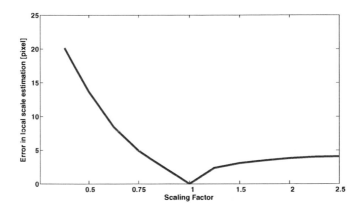

Figure 2.15. The stability of our shape-centered interest points against scale changes. The x-Axis denotes the scaling factor between the original image and the image on which scales were estimated. The y-Axis shows the average difference between the two estimated scales. Our scale estimation is very robust and, especially with respect to magnification, it can compensate large scale changes without errors larger than 5 pixels.

mation at our interest points, we applied them in a scale-invariant object detection task [41]. Such a real-world task has the advantage of providing insight into the performance of the features in more complex systems as opposed to the rather abstract evaluations illustrated here.

2.4.1 Scale-Invariant Object Detection

We now validate the scale-invariance of our SCIP within a pedestrian detection task. Since pedestrians can appear in a large variety of scales and poses, this is a very challenging problem and it has received considerable attention from the computer vision community lately [1, 40, 52, 82, 111]. We want to stress that we use pedestrian detection only to demonstrate and compare the scale-invariance of our features. We do not aim at providing a state-of-the-art pedestrian detection algorithm.

Pedestrian detection is an important open problem in computer vision

35

Medial Feature ISM

The ISM is a generalization of the Hough transformation

As an algorithmic back-end for pedestrian detection, we modified the Implicit Shape Model (ISM) [83, 82] to accommodate our features. The ISM has proved to be a powerful tool for simultaneous object-detection and segmentation. The basic idea of the ISM is a generalization of the Hough transformation (see [5, 39]).

Object position is estimated relative to locally detected features in a probabilistic framework

We are given an extracted image patch $\mathbf{e}$ (which is the local evidence) observed at the image location $l \in \mathbb{R}^2$. We are interested in the probability distribution over possible object positions $\mathbf{x} \in \mathbb{R}^2$ and scales $s \in \mathbb{R}$ given the evidence $p(\mathbf{x}, s \mid \mathbf{e}, l)$. Since this would be computationally infeasible, we approximate the probability density using discrete votes. By matching it to a codebook of learned local appearances, we obtain a set of interpretations I_k of the patch $p(I_k \mid \mathbf{e}, l)$. If a codebook entry matches the evidence, it casts several votes $p(\mathbf{x}, s \mid \mathbf{e}, I_k, l)$ for possible object positions $\mathbf{x}$ and scales s. Summing over all interpretations of the patch yields the following marginalization:

$$p(\mathbf{x}, s \mid \mathbf{e}, l) = \sum_k p(\mathbf{x}, s \mid \mathbf{e}, I_k, l) p(I_k \mid \mathbf{e}, l). \qquad (2.11)$$

Since, I_k are the interpretations of the image patch we can treat the first term as independent of $\mathbf{e}$. Furthermore, by applying the codebook matching scheme independent of the location in the image we can simplify the equation to

$$p(\mathbf{x}, s \mid \mathbf{e}, l) = \sum_k p(\mathbf{x}, s \mid I_k, l) p(I_k \mid \mathbf{e}). \qquad (2.12)$$

The first term reflects the Hough votes for possible object positions and scales given an interpretation and location of a patch. The second term is the quality of the match between the interpretation and the evidence.

36

By integrating over all N patches $\mathbf{e}_i$ at locations l_i, which were extracted from the image, the final probability density in the voting space is derived

$$p(\mathbf{x}, s) = \frac{\sum_{i=1}^{N} p(\mathbf{x}, s \mid \mathbf{e}_i, l_i)}{Z}, \qquad (2.13)$$

where Z is a normalization factor, which ensures that the equation sums to one. The intuition behind this equation is that if the algorithm detects a foot somewhere in the image and a head in a plausible position relative to it, those two will vote for the same correct pedestrian-center while all other votes will not amplify each other (see Figure 2.16 for illustrations).

Initially, we obtain a codebook of local appearances by drawing patches from the edge map at SCIPs and clustering them using the k-means algorithm. We then go through the training database and find all matches of our codebook entries $\mathbf{e}_i$ using the normalized cross correlation (NCC) as a similarity measure and a threshold of 0.7 to identify matches. At the matching positions, we store the relative position (dx, dy) of the object center with relation to the interest point and the relative difference in our scale estimates (see Equation 2.8) denoted by ds. Following this scheme we obtain a set of votes $v_{i,k} = (dx_k, dy_k, ds_k)$ for each interest point i, where k is the index of the vote. In the ensuing detection phase we look for matches between our codebook entries and the SCIPs in the image and cast the discrete votes $v(i, k)$ for possible object centers and scales in a 3D voting space. This voting space is a discrete approximation of Equation 2.13 making the problem of finding a maximum of the density function computationally feasible.

Discrete approximation of the probability density using a set of votes per codebook patch

Early versions of the ISM did not include a scale estimation. We include a local scale estimation step meaning that we have to scale all votes accordingly (a head that is identified at double the size as in the codebook will be twice as far away from the cen-

Local scale estimation greatly improves the ISM

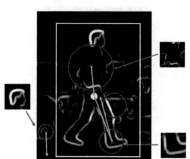

Figure 2.16. The medial feature implicit shape model used for our scale invariance evaluation. The red dots and circles are the found SCIPs with their associated local scales. The patches aside the edge map are codebook entries. Blue arrows indicate matches between interest points and codebook entries. Green Arrows are the votes that are associated with the codebook entries. Finding the largest cluster of votes will yield the center (yellow dot) and the bounding box of the pedestrian (yellow box).

ter of the person in pixel). Including the local scale estimation of our features as a preprocessing step for the template matching has two advantages: First, it allows to capture a greater variety of unique local appearances in a codebook of the same size, because patches from the same object part at different sizes can be clustered together. Second, it allows the template matching scheme to generalize to a wide range of yet unseen scales as will be demonstrated in the next Section.

Finding the modes of the voting space using the mean-shift algorithm

We now have to find the maximum density in the discrete $3D$ voting space $p(\mathbf{x}, s)$. Following the proposed approach of Leibe et al. [83] we do this using the mean shift mode search [27]. Mean shift is an unsupervised non-parametric clustering scheme similar to k-means, but it has the advantage of not requiring a priori knowledge about the number of clusters in the dataset. Mean shift uses local density estimation to iteratively merge together data points until convergence and has been recognized as a valuable technique for tracking [164], segmentation [158] and object detection [84]. The modes returned by the mean shift clustering are hypotheses about possible centers and scales of pedestrians in the image that are supported by several interest points. For a more detailed explanation of the ISM algorithm, confer to e.g. Leibe et al. [82].

Evaluation

To evaluate the stability of our features against scale changes directly, we train the ISM on images containing pedestrians of a fixed size and evaluate its detection performance on images containing persons of a different size. This allows us to measure the ability of the algorithm to transfer knowledge gained at one scale to a different one. The broader the range of scales to which the algorithm is able to generalize to, the more information can be shared between even distant scales. This in turn will allow for more compact codebooks and more robust object representations.

Evaluation of the ability to transfer knowledge between different scales

Figure 2.17. Examples from our computer-generated database (three pictures on the left) and the INRIA pedestrian database [33] (three images on the right), respectively.

We used two datasets for evaluation. The first one consists of 3D avatars driven by motion capture data, which were inserted into clutter using alpha-blending (Figure 2.17 (left)). It includes 56 images for each, training and testing. In the second one, we took images from the INRIA pedestrian database [33] containing only one single upright person, allowing us to fix the size of the pedestrians (Figure 2.17(right)). This dataset is comprised of 100 images for training and 87 for testing.

Testing is done on an artificial and a real world dataset of pedestrians in clutter

Comparison of the scale-invariance of SCIP and SIFT

We compare the scale-invariance properties of three methods: Our medial features, the SIFT keypoint detector [92], which also yields a local scale estimation, and, as a baseline, we evaluate our medial features with a fixed local scale of 50 pixel, which is approximately the mean of all estimated local scales across the database. Since the two interest point detectors produce very different codebooks, we limit the codebook sizes to 400 entries to keep them comparable. The maximal number of votes per codebook entry is limited to 50 by selecting votes at random if the limit is exceeded. We use edge patches drawn from an edge energy map as descriptor. The detection rates at different scales on both databases are reported in Figure 2.18.

SCIP scale estimation outperforms or matches SIFT scale estimation

This Figure demonstrates that our features provide a useful shape description in artificial and real world images with difficult background clutter even with a small codebook of only 400 entries. Furthermore, it is shown that the algorithm benefits greatly from the scale estimation the more the scale factor differs from one . Without scale estimation we see worst performance, especially on the challenging real world imagery. Both graphs demonstrate that our medial features perform comparably to SIFT-based keypoints and depending on the dataset may even outperform them.

2.4.2 Image Encoding Using SCIPs

Evaluation of the encoded image information in an edge map reconstruction task

Image encoding by expressing the image as a list of interest points and descriptors is an important but lossy step in computer vision. In this Section, we quantify the portion of image information that is lost during this step. We investigate this using an edge map reconstruction task based on a codebook of visual words drawn from SCIPs and edge-based interest points (in our case SIFT) .

Unsupervised creation of a codebook of edge-map patches

Our dataset consists of 50 images for training and 50 for testing taken from the Berkely Segmentation Dataset [100], which contains natural photographs in combination with human segmentations (a

40

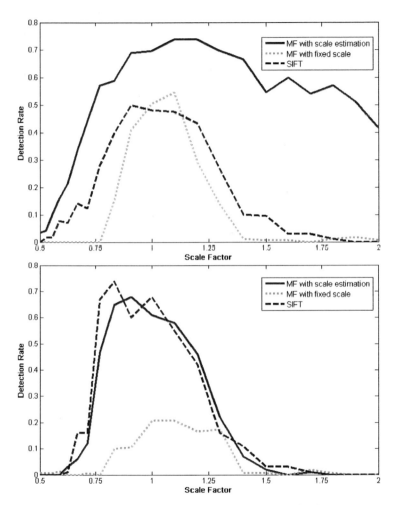

Figure 2.18. Detection rates on the computer generated (top) and on the INRIA database (bottom) over size scale ratio training vs. test images.

Figure 2.19. The edge map reconstruction pipeline. Patches are extracted from the edge map and compared to a codebook. The matching patches are rendered onto a canvas. Images on the right represent reconstruction from SCIP, corner-based and mixed codebooks.

more detailed explanation of the dataset will follow in Chapter 4). In a first step, we created a codebook of square edge map patches from the training image set. This codebook is obtained by extracting patches at SCIP and SIFT interest points using the estimated scales and orientations of both resulting in scale and rotation-invariant patches. To reduce redundancies in the codebook, we performed an agglomerative clustering using normalized cross correlation (NCC) as a similarity measure. We obtained the final codebooks by k-means clustering where k is the fixed size of the particular codebook.

SCIPs can encode a larger portion of the original edge map

In the reconstruction phase, we matched our codebook entries to the interest points found in images from the test set. If the normalized cross correlation is above the threshold of 0.7 we rendered the stored edge map patch from the codebook onto a canvas. The reconstruction pipeline is depicted in Figure 2.19. We used the euclidean distance between original and reconstructed edge map as performance measure. Figure 2.20 (left) shows the performance for different codebook sizes. For practical codebook sizes, reconstruction based on SCIP codebooks outperforms SIFT. For very small codebook sizes, SIFT yielded better edge map reconstructions. This is to be expected since SIFT is edge-based, which seems to be initially preferable for the task. However, as the code-

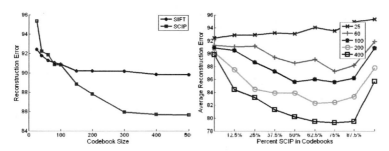

Figure 2.20. Edge map reconstruction performance. **Left:** Mean euclidean distance of the original edge maps to the reconstructed edge maps for SIFT and SCIP as interest point detectors. **Right:** The reconstruction performance using mixtures of both codebooks. The legend denotes the overall codebook size.

books get bigger the reconstruction based on medial features starts to outperform SIFT.

In a second experiment, we evaluated the edge map reconstruction using mixed codebooks. We reconstructed the edge map from both kinds of interest points at different ratios to one another and fused them by calculating the weighted average. The total size of the mixed codebook was kept constant and just the percentage of SCIP patches in it changed. No optimization of the combination is performed. The performances are shown in Figure 2.20 (right). The combination of shape-centered and corner-based interest points clearly outperform the codebooks from a single source. This indicates that medial features and SIFT encode different kinds of information and that a combination of both might be useful for computer vision algorithms. Since they are shape-centered, SCIPs also offer a direct way to encode the color of the shape. This fact can be used to reconstruct the original image (instead of just the edge map) or augment feature vectors to avoid tracking ambiguities.

SCIPs and corner-interest points encode complementary information

43

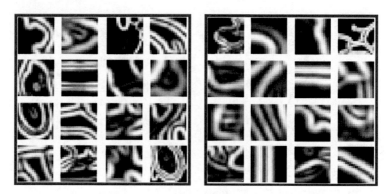

Figure 2.21. Examples of SCIP (blue box) and SIFT (red box) patches drawn from the Caltech 101 database which contains natural images.

Information Carried by Shape Centered Features

The edge map reconstruction task in the previous Section already hinted at the fact that shape-centered and edge-based interest points denote two different channels of information. In this Section, we will provide further evidence for that observation.

Sampling of quadratic patches at SCIP and SIFT interest points

We randomly sampled 100 SIFTs and SCIPs together with their estimated local scales on images from the Caltech101 database [45, 46]. We then extracted quadratic patches at the interest points from the edge maps of the images. We used the squared sum of two orthogonal Gabor filters as edge operator. Examples of the SIFT and SCIP patches can be seen in Figure 2.21.

MDS of SIFT and SCIP demonstrate that they occur at structurally different locations

We apply a multidimensional scaling (MDS) [15, 149] algorithm to resulting patches. MDS is a statistical technique to generate a low-dimensional embedding that preserves the similarities or dissimilarities of the data, in order to visualize its structure. Figure 2.22 shows a two-dimensional embedding computed by MDS. The euclidean distance between the edge-map patches was employed to create the pairwise similarity matrix.

44

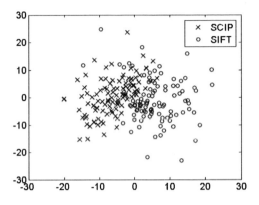

Figure 2.22.
MDS clustering:
The two
codebooks are
located at two
distinct clusters
in the latent
MDS space
indicating the
complementary
nature of edge
based and
shape-centered
interest points.

2.5   Conclusion and Outlook

In this Chapter we have presented a novel set of shape-centered interest points called SCIP. They are formed at locations of high local symmetry and are therefore largely invariant against background clutter. The interest points are detected as the local maxima of the flux flow $\mathcal{F}$ of the normalized gradient vector flow field V_N. This approach makes them much more robust against clutter than the standard approach to extracting shape-centered interest points using the distance transformation. By scanning outwards from the SCIPs and finding the salient edges that led to their formation, we can estimate a local scale and orientation at the interest points. The local scale and orientation allows higher-level vision algorithms to detect the interest point associated with a shape after rescaling and rotation, making the SCIPs scale and rotation-invariant. In the evaluation in Section 2.4, we demonstrated that the SCIPs are comparably powerful to state-of-the-art interest point detectors. We furthermore showed that the interest points encode different and to some extend complementary image

45

information.

Future lines of research include the extension of the framework to dynamic scenes. Tracking of interest points in tandem with the local scale estimation can be used to detect looming patterns (as shown by Curio and Engel [32]) and extensions to this idea could provide high-level information such as objects with independent motion and time-to-contact.

3

Mid-Level Shape Encoding

The clever combatant looks to the effect of combined
energy, and does not require too much from individuals.

Sun Tzu - The Art of War

The shape-centered interest points that were introduced in the
previous Chapter are highly-localized, low-level, bottom-up features. They are already powerful image descriptors, but the unique
strength of medial features is that they can be used as a tool to
integrate information about their associated shape from a wider
range of sources. By accumulating information in their surroundings, they act as mid-level features of intermediate complexity.
Such mid-level features encode not only local image properties,
but carry information about a larger area of the image and can
encode the spatial relationships of other, low-level features in the
vicinity. This ability to integrate information and preprocess the
image to obtain representations of higher descriptive power sepa-
rates medial features from purely low-level features such as SIFT.
They differ from higher-level features (e.g. the Scene GIST descrip-

Medial features
can integrate
information from
their surroundings
and provide
powerful mid-level
shape descriptors

47

tor [112, 113]) by still being localized and associated with single shape entities in the image.

Feature grouping and medial feature superpixels are two such mid-level representations

In this Chapter, we introduce two approaches, which exploit these properties of medial features and yield powerful mid-level representations for computer vision applications. In Section 3.1, we demonstrate how medial features can be used to group or link together corner interest points as shown by Engel and Curio [42]. This scheme yields powerful meta-features that combine the descriptive power of corner interest points with the advantages of SCIPs (e.g. a direct association with a single shape and robustness against noise and clutter). In Section 3.2, we propose a segmentation scheme based on our medial features that divides the image into small, visually uniform areas (see Engel et al. [41]). Our approach falls in the category of a bottom-up (ergo without any knowledge about the objects in the image) oversegmentation, which is often called a *superpixel* segmentation. Such oversegementations have been shown to be very useful in high-level computer vision. As our superpixels are based on medial features, they offer excellent properties, for instance, close alignment with salient edges in the image. This allows them to outperform other state-of-the-art superpixel segmentation techniques.

3.1 Feature Grouping

Bottom-up grouping of corner interest points at SCIPs

In the presence of noise and clutter, the information available at individual interest points, be it shape-centered interest points or edge-based ones, can be seriously degraded. In an object recognition task, for example, interest points can be spurious (e.g. they are located at positions determined by clutter or noise, which have not occurred in the training set) or the descriptors associated with the interest points can be unrecognizable i.e. the interest point has formed at an informative location but the descriptor is influenced

48

by the noise such that it cannot be matched to a known descriptor from the training dataset. To address this problem, we perform a bottom-up grouping step in which interest points that likely belong to the same shape are clustered together. It is vital to notice that our grouping is performed in a bottom-up manner without any requirement for detailed object knowledge. More complex schemes that include top-down feedback mechanisms might be better able to cluster together interest points belonging to one object, but they notoriously run into a chicken-egg problem: To know which interest points should be clustered it is necessary to know the object category, but to reliably determine the object category it is necessary to know which interest points belong to it. Our bottom-up mechanism circumvents this problem by grouping together features that belong to one shape. If we can ensure that the shape is a subregion of an object and does not cross object-boundaries, such grouped features can encode much more valuable information about the local shape than the single features by themselves while also providing robustness against noise and clutter.

In the following Sections, we propose a novel technique for image feature linking that has been put forward by Engel and Curio [42]. The algorithm is based on the feature extraction pipeline by Engel and Curio [41] (see Section 2.2), which we have adopted for our novel grouping approach. Section 3.1.2 describes how the GVF field and shape-centered interest points can be used to link edge-based corner features. In Section 3.1.4, we evaluate our approach by comparing the descriptor strength of grouped SCIPs and SIFTs in a classification task.

3.1.1 State of the Art

In biologically plausible computer vision systems features of intermediate complexity have been learned from low-level image features [138], building upon the biologically motivated approach of

Riesenhuber and Poggio [129] for hierarchical object recognition. Gestalt law principles have been explicitly implemented for grouping features within recognition architectures, e.g. [13]. A similar approach has been proposed that incorporates these principles into the design of Markov Random Field structures [165] that are based on the FORMS (Flexible Object Recognition and Modeling System) shape recognition system [166].

Traditionally, perceptual grouping was most interested in linking and clustering of features and edges and there exist a wide variety of approaches to this end, e.g. the contour completion work of Stahle et al. [146] and Ren et al. [127]. A different current interpretation of the grouping problem is to use superpixels to cluster together SIFTs and other local image information(e.g. [66, 120]). These approaches usually sample SIFT descriptors densely at different scales inside a superpixel and build a histogram of their occurrences after quantization using an optimized codebook. As SIFT descriptors were designed to work in tandem with the SIFT corner detector, such approaches often run into problems with highly redundant information yielded by keypoints that lie too close together. Another very interesting approach along those lines by Fulkerson et al. [51] aims to integrate information of surrounding superpixels and use this information as descriptor for a central superpixel. Our approach circumvents this problem by not relying on dense sampling of SIFT descriptors and not depending on a specific superpixel segmentation strategy.

3.1.2 Grouping Corner-Based Features

The GVF field provides the necessary information for the correct linking

We now describe how we use the shape-centered interest points to group together corner-based interest points such as SIFT. We exploit the properties of the underlying GVF field to link the corner-based SIFTs with their strong edge-descriptors to the medial features. We show that this linking yields an even stronger descriptor

50

Figure 3.1. Shape-centered interest points (green circle) are directly linked to a single shape while corner interest points (yellow dot) are formed at the intersection between shapes. The corner interest point belongs to the car, the tree, and the background at the same time.

for the shape-centered interest points in Section 3.1.4. We compare the power of the linked-descriptors to the information contained at the corner points alone in a multi-class classification task.

Corner interest points are formed at locations with a rich edge structure, thus providing very powerful and uniquely identifiable descriptors. However, they suffer from the drawback that they are located at the edges between two shapes making it hard to associate them with one shape in e.g. a classification task (see example in Figure 3.1). Our shape-centered interest points have the benefit of being tightly associated with one specific shape, but suffer from the drawback that there is only scarce local edge information. By combining the advantages of both approaches, we can provide strong descriptors at locations that are connected to one unique Sshape.

> Grouping results in a combination of powerful descriptors and tight connection to a unique shape

The normalized GVF field V_N provides an unique gradient direction for each image location (see Figure 3.2 (middle)). The shape-centered interest points are located at the shock loci of the field. Starting at corner interest points we follow the vectors in the GVF field (c.f. Figure 3.2(right)). This procedure will converge to the local maxima of the flux flow field $\mathcal{F}$.

> V_N provides paths from the corners to the SCIPs

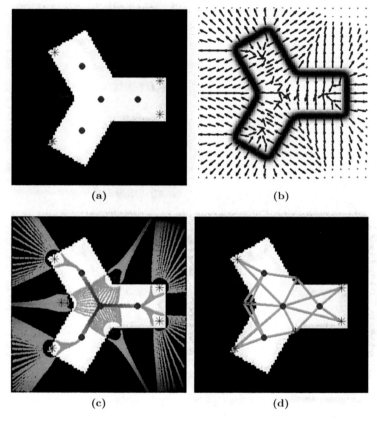

Figure 3.2. a) Example with SCIP (blue) and SIFT (red) interest points.
b) The GVF field superimposed on the edge map. **c)** Evolution of the traces
$T_{i,n}$ overlayed on the image (Color gradient green to red indicates iteration
steps of the traces). **d)** SIFTs linked (green lines) to the SCIPs.

Equation 3.1 demonstrates the idea of iteratively following the normalized GVF field using a trace T. Here, a trace is a series of $2D$ image positions leading from a corner to a SCIP. Because there might be multiple medial feature interest points associated with a corner, we have to follow the GVF field in all directions. To reach all adjacent maxima of $\mathcal{F}$, we generate 36 traces $T_{i,0}$ ($i \in 1..36$) at $10°$ intervals on a ring with radius 5 pixel around the edge-based corner point (see Figure 3.2 (c)). We then propagate the trace along the gradients as determined by the GVF field:

Traces T link the corners to SCIPs in all directions

$$T_{i,n+1} = T_{i,n} + V_N(T_{i,n}), \qquad (3.1)$$

where $T_{i,n+1}$ is the updated position of the ith trace after $n+1$ iterations. Because of numerical issues or noise, the traces might not completely reach all shape-centered interest points. To address this issue, we connect the corner interest point to the SCIP as soon as a traces arrives in the disc with the radius of the estimated local scale S around the interest point. Figure 3.2 shows traces of SIFT interest points in the GVF field while drifting toward the medial features.

The temporal evolution of traces

This grouping algorithm usually converges after $30 - 50$ iterations. The scheme can be significantly sped up by terminating traces that have reached a local minimum and by combining traces that have converged (i.e. delete $T_{i,n}$ if $T_{i,n} = T_{j,k}$ for any $k < n$ and $i \neq j$). Following this algorithm, we obtain a bipartite graph (see Figure 3.2 D) of groupings between corner and medial feature interest points.

Terminating traces that have converged yields substantial speedups

$$G(C, M, E) \text{ with edges } e_{i,j} \in E \qquad (3.2)$$

$$e_{i,j} = \begin{cases} 1 & \text{if there is a trace from corner } C_i \text{ to SCIP } M_j \\ 0 & \text{otherwise} \end{cases} \qquad (3.3)$$

3.1.3   Similarity Measures for Grouped Features

After the grouping described above we obtain a complex descriptor D at each SCIP that consists of the descriptors of the surrounding corner interest points:

$$D = [Q_1, Q_2, .., Q_n],\qquad(3.4)$$

where Q_i are the descriptors at the SIFTs connected to the current interest point. As D integrates information from several corner interest points (e.g. SIFTs), it is robust against noise and clutter that might occur at the single SIFTs. However, for the descriptor D to be useful, it needs to carry valuable information but must also provide a way to compute the similarity to another descriptor of the same kind. Such similarity judgments are an integral component of every machine learning and computer vision system, as they allow to decide whether two shapes belong to the same or different classes. Therefore, we need a similarity or distance measure d between two grouped features:

$$\text{similarity} = d\,(D_1, D_2)\qquad(3.5)$$

In the case of comparing e.g. SIFTs that provide a fixed-length descriptor, defining a distance measure is straight forward, such as using the euclidean distance or in the case of e.g. color histograms using the earth movers distance (EMD). In the present case, the problem is more difficult as the cardinalities of the descriptors D_1 and D_2 might be different (i.e. two SCIPs might have different numbers of SIFTs linked to them). Defining a distance or similarity measure between sets of interest points with different cardinalities is notoriously difficult. It has been noted that the triangular inequality does not generally hold in shape similarity comparison of this kind [10].

Descriptor at SCIP consists just of the grouped corner interest points

A similarity measure between descriptors of different cardinality

The easiest way to approach the problem of comparing two sets of features with different cardinalities is to use a *bag of visual words* approach (e.g. [30, 57]). This is a common technique in computer vision often used to compare images that can contain different numbers of interest points. The idea is to select a fixed number N of exemplar descriptors C_i, which can be learned from training data using k-Means [94, 147] or a similar clustering technique. Then, each element Q_i of the descriptor D is associated with the most similar entry C_j in the codebook C. By counting how often each codebook entry C_j was the closest one to all grouped interest points in D, we obtain a histogram frequency H_j for entry j (a scalar value). Combining all H_j's gives us the bag of visual words descriptor H:

(margin note: Codebook of visual words approach)

$$H = [H_1, H_2, \ldots, H_N] \tag{3.6}$$

As the histograms have a fixed size N (each H_j is a scalar so the dimensionality equals the number of entries C_j in the codebook) we are are now able to compare two sets of grouped features despite their different cardinalities by e.g. computing the euclidean distance between the two associated histograms. However, experiments using a codebook of visual words approach demonstrated that this approach is not applicable in our case. There are only 46 connected SIFTs linked to each SCIP on average. Even with a moderately sized codebook of only a few hundred entries, this would lead to feature vectors with only few non-zero entries, making distance judgments between the graphs noisy and unreliable, thus sacrificing the advantage of the grouping approach.

(margin note: Histograms would be too sparse for meaningful distance judgments in our case)

We therefore opted to perform the distance judgments using a modified SIFT matching scheme. We compare two sets of features D_1 and D_2 by first calculating the pairwise euclidean distances between all corner interest points to obtain the distance/similarity matrix S:

(margin note: SIFT matching scheme between the graphs)

$$S_{i,j} = |Q_{1,i}, Q_{2,j}|, \qquad (3.7)$$

Count unique matches between two sets of SIFTs

where $Q_{1,i}$ is the i'th SIFT descriptor linked to the first SCIP and $Q_{2,j}$ is the j'th SIFT descriptor linked to the second SCIP. We then count the number of valid matches between the smaller of the two graphs (we take it to be D_1 without loss of generality) to the larger of the two graphs. We accept two SIFTs from the two graphs as matches if and only if the ratio of the distance between the best and the second best match is smaller than 0.8 (see Equation 3.8):

$$Q_{1,p} \text{ and } Q_{2,q} \text{ match iff } \frac{|Q_{1,p}, Q_{2,q}|}{|Q_{1,p}, Q_{2,n}|} < 0.8 \quad \forall n \neq q \qquad (3.8)$$

Subgraph matching could yield a different distance measure

This scheme has been proposed by Lowe [92] and avoids having to set a threshold for matches in euclidean distance, which does not work very well. Another approach to calculate the distance between the two sets of features comes from graph matching and is based on subgraph matching [110]. Yet, this method requires several training and optimization steps to establish a useful set of subgraphs making it less applicable for our bottom-up feature extraction pipeline.

3.1.4 Evaluation

Performance in 8-class recognition task to measure strength of descriptor

We now evaluate the information available at SIFTs (i.e. their descriptor) vs. the available information at SCIPs after the grouping described in the previous Section. For this purpose, we ignore all other information available directly at the SCIPs (such as color or structure of the flux field $\mathcal{F}$) and rely only on the descriptors from the grouped SIFTs. To this end, we extract SIFTs and link them to our medial features on images from the StreetScenes database [14]. This database contains more than 3500 images taken in Boston with associated labels for eight classes (Pedestrian, Bicycle, Car,

56

Street, Sidewalk, Building, Sky, Tree). An example image from the database with linked interest points is shown in Figure 3.3.

To demonstrate the power of feature grouping by medial features, we perform a recognition task with eight classes. We randomly sample 200 SIFT interest points and 200 SCIPs with the connected SIFT interest points for each of the 8 classes (car, pedestrians, building, ...) from the images. This yields a combined training dataset with 1600 SIFT descriptors for the corner classification task and 1600 graphs of SIFT features grouped at SCIPs for the medial feature classification task.

Sample 200 SIFT and 200 SCIP per class from the StreetScenes database

In the next step, we use the well-known *k Nearest Neighbors* (kNN) classifier (with $k = 5$) for classification. The simplicity of the classifier is chosen deliberately to minimize any effects of training and parameter estimation on the results. We use the euclidean distance between the SIFTs and the distance described in Section 3.1.3 to measure distances between grouped SCIPs. We can now apply the kNN algorithm to classify SIFTs and SCIPs (based solely on the grouped SIFTs). Our test set contains 200 examples for each of the classes for each type of interest point. The classification rates for each class are shown in Figure 3.4. The Figure clearly demonstrates that SCIPs outperform SIFTs in terms of classification rates for seven of the classes and equally for 'sky'.

Using kNN for classification minimizes possible training biases

We want to stress that at both types of interest points only the descriptors from the SIFT interest points are available, i.e. both have to rely on the same information. Yet, by linking the SIFT information in a purely feed-forward manner at the shape-centered interest points we gain a more powerful description of the local image structure. Further increases in performance would be possible by augmenting the descriptor at the medial features by local color, shape and texture information or by introducing geometric constraints in the distance measure between two graphs.

Both kinds of interest points only have access to SIFT descriptors for classification

(a)

(b)

Figure 3.3. Image from the StreetScenes database [14] with SIFT (red) and SCIP (blue) features. **Top:** Overlay of the groupings from the SIFTs to the SCIPs on the image. **Bottom:** Grouping of SIFTs to SCIPs (each line color represents the graph associated with one SCIP). The image has been downscaled to reduce the number of interest points.

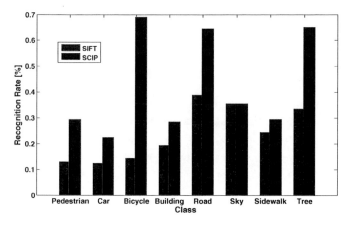

Figure 3.4. The classification rates for SIFTs (blue) and SCIPs (red). SCIPs were classified solely based on the grouped SIFTs. The mean recognition rates across all classes are 24% for SIFT and 43% for SCIP. The baseline of random guessing is 12.5%.

3.1.5 Conclusion and Outlook

In this Section, we have presented a novel way to group together corner interest points (specifically SIFT) at the shape-centered interest points introduced in the previous Chapter. We employed the properties of the normalized GVF field and the estimated local scale to link corners to the medial features using a simulated drifting process. This grouping yields a powerful mid-level shape-centered representation of the local image structure. It furthermore provides a strong descriptor for the SCIP, thus overcoming their main weakness. We have shown the usefulness of the approach in a classification task on a dataset composed of natural images.

Future research could aim to augment the descriptors by the local color and flux field structure available at the SCIP. Furthermore, we could exploit the fact that the SCIPs are tightly connected to one shape in the image to disambiguate the information at the SIFT corners. By suppressing the part of SIFT descriptor that encodes edges belonging to a different shape (for SIFTs that were formed along the edge between two shapes), the specificity of the descriptors could be greatly enhanced.

One limitation that remains is that such schemes only operate on localized interest points and encode pixels between these points only implicitly via the descriptors. An approach that accounts for all pixels in the image simultaneously is presented in the next Section.

3.2   Medial Feature Superpixel

Pixels are not natural entities of images but are a consequence of the quantized representations involved in acquiring images and they consequently carry only very little information by themselves. Also, the number of pixels grows quickly with respect to resolution. To address this problem, segmentation techniques are used that group together homogeneous clusters of pixels. If the pixels are combined in a purely feed-forward manner (i.e. without any object knowledge), an oversegmentation of the image called *superpixels* is obtained.

Pixels are not natural entities but artifacts of the image generation process

In this Section, we present a superpixel segmentation methodology described by Engel et al. [43] that makes use of the medial feature transform described in Section 2.2 (based on the Medial Features of Engel et al. [41]). We use the flux flow field $\mathcal{F}$ introduced in Section 2.2 to create seeds for the segmentation process. We expand the seeds to a full oversegmentation of the image with the watershed algorithm using $\mathcal{F}$ as a height map. To evaluate the performance of the proposed algorithm, we employ the Berkeley Segmentation Dataset [100] and compare the performance of our algorithm to the two state-of-the-art approaches of Felzenszwalb and Huttenlocher [47] as well as Ren and Malik [128].

Superpixels based on the medial features from Chapter 2

In Section 3.2.2, we employ the Medial Features introduced in Section 2.2 to create an oversegmentation of an image. Section 3.2.3 reports on our evaluation and the performance of the superpixel. Lastly, Section 3.2.4 presents a short conclusion and an outlook for this Section.

3.2.1   State of the Art

Oversegmentation techniques have long been recognized as useful devices to create powerful mid-level representations of images for computer vision. Early methods for obtaining such superpixels include e.g. region merging techniques such as [29], approaches mapping image pixels to a feature space using mean-shift [28], and methods based on spectral clustering [160].

One state-of-the-art method for superpixel segmentation was introduced by Ren and Malik [128], who employ a Normalized Cut criterion [139] to recursively partition an image using contour and texture cues. Another popular approach has been proposed by Felzenszwalb and Huttenlocher [47], using an efficient graph-based representation of local neighborhoods. A third application to obtain superpixels are the so-called Turbopixels introduced by Levinshtein et al. [88]. They obtain an evenly spaced oversegmentation by starting with a regular grid of seeds and propagating the superpixel boundaries along the geometric flow in the image. Superpixels have proved to be very useful and several applications that employ superpixel representations exist. Recent noteworthy works include depth from single images [134], human pose estimation [109] and general scene understanding [66].

3.2.2 Creating Superpixels

Use thresholded $\mathcal{F}$ to generate seed areas for the superpixels

The core idea behind oversegmentation algorithms is to find and group together regions that are uniform in their appearance. The medial features described in the earlier Sections provide a means to this end by being formed at the centers of regions of uniform appearance. We take advantage of the points of high symmetry, denoted by the medial features, by using them as seeds for the oversegmentation. To obtain these seeds, we threshold the flux flow field $\mathcal{F}$ with θ and assign unique labels to the connected areas. The GVF field is the first step of calculating the medial features

The optimal edge operator is task-dependent

and operates on an edge image E. Choosing the right edge detector to create E is task-dependent. Evaluations showed that the thresholded Sobel edge operator performs very well in the context of oversegmentation. More intricate edge detectors such as Canny

62

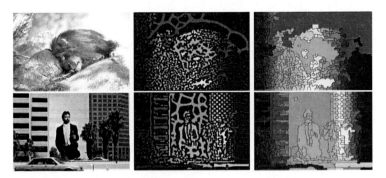

Figure 3.5. Two examples of the seed structure and superpixel segmentation. **Left:** Original image from the Berkeley Segmentation Database [100]. **Center:** Connected seed areas after thresholding the flux flow field $\mathcal{F}$. **Right:** Superpixel segmentation after applying the watershed algorithm.

[21] can suppress fine edge details. However, this is not desirable for our application, since creating too many segments is less harmful than prematurely merging segments belonging to two different regions. Furthermore, the GVF will eliminate spurious edge pixels that are potentially created by the less complex edge detector, allowing a stable formation of the seeds for the oversegmentation. An example of the seed structure after thresholding the medial features is shown in Figure 3.5 (middle row). To avoid problems in large uniform areas, it should be assured that the GVF field has fully converged in the whole image.

To complete the oversegmentation, we need to assign the remaining pixels (pixels not in the seed areas), which are not included in the seeds, to coherent regions. For this purpose, we apply the watershed algorithm proposed by Meyer et al. [103] for which efficient implementations are available. The algorithm operates on a height map and simulates successive flooding of the relief, starting from the seeds set in the image. Borders or 'watersheds' are formed where the rising water of two different basins meet (see

Watershed algorithm distributes the pixels between seed areas

63

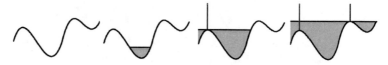

Figure 3.6. An intuitive 1D example of the watershed algorithm. A height map (in our case the flux flow $\mathcal{F}$) is flooded by a rising waterline (blue). Where two basins of rising water meet, a watershed (red) of infinite height is erected. The resulting red lines form the final superpixel segmentation.

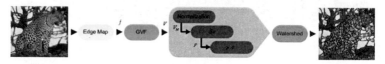

Figure 3.7. Overview of the processing pipeline for medial feature oversegmentation. The GVF field V is computed on the edge map. After normalization of V and the computation of the flux flow $\mathcal{F}$, the seeds are obtained by thresholding with θ. Starting from the seeds, the watershed is computed using $\mathcal{F}$ as a height map.

Figure 3.6). As a height map, we use the flux flow image $\mathcal{F}$. As an outcome of the GVF optimization process, $\mathcal{F}$ preserves the salient edge information (local minima, negative) complementary to the formed symmetries (local maxima, positive). Thus, this approach preserves the edge structure of the original image, which is critical for an oversegmentation algorithm. This preservation of the underlying edge structure presents also an advantage over a simple creation of a Voronoi diagram extended from the seeds, which would be another way to create the superpixels from initial seeds. Our pipeline for superpixel segmentation is depicted in Figure 3.7.

3.2.3 Evaluation

We compare our oversegmentation method with two state-of-the-art approaches. The first one is an extension of the superpixel algorithm proposed by Felzenszwalb and Huttenlocher [47] and the second one is the method proposed by Ren and Malik [128], which is based on normalized graph cuts. As a baseline method, we show the performance of a standard watershed method computed on Canny edge maps. We measure the performance of the over-segmentation algorithms on the Berkeley Segmentation Dataset [100], which contains 300 images (200 in the training data set and 100 in the test set) with several human drawn segmentations for each image (an example from the database is shown in Figure 3.8). Participants were told to segment the images in as many regions as they wanted. No explicit definitions of 'region' or 'segment' were given ensuring that participants would rely on their intuitive understanding of these concepts. As a result, the human-made segmentations differ greatly between subjects, with the number of segments per image ranging from 5 to over 30. Apart from the differences between the segmentations, human observers further-more rely on their vast experience with natural images and their knowledge of image semantics. This knowledge is not available to bottom-up segmentation algorithms, thus rendering the auto-matic reconstruction of human segmentations a very difficult and ambiguous challenge.

Evaluation against state-of-the-art algorithms on the Berkeley Segmentation dataset

Consequently, superpixel algorithms do not aim to fully explain human segmentations. They only try to provide a more compact image representation that can serve as a starting point for higher-level segmentation algorithms. Such higher-level algorithms can then merge superpixels into larger regions and reconstruct human-like image segmentations based on learned relationships. However, should the superpixel segmentation already cross borders between

Optimally, superpixels should not cross object-boundaries

65

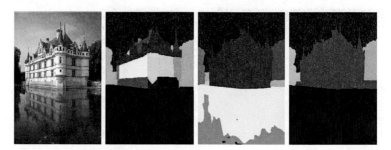

Figure 3.8. Example image from the Berkeley Segmentation Dataset [100] (left) and three human segmentation results. Note the different levels of detail in the human segmentations, which indicates that semantic segmentation is a difficult and ambiguous process even for humans (e.g. how many separate parts does the castle consist of). This poses the question if a ground-truth segmentation even exists or if there might be a multitude of correct answers.

human-made segments, an algorithm based on merging regions would necessarily fail. Thus, to correctly evaluate oversegmentation algorithms, we have to use a performance measure that tells us how well a higher-level algorithm *could* be able to reconstruct the human segmentation. Consequently, our performance measure penalizes segments of the oversegmentation that cross the borders of the target shape. On the other hand, it is desirable to end up with a small number of segments to reduce the complexity of the subsequent merging or classification problems. Based on these observations, we formulated the following performance measure:

$$P = \frac{\sum_{i=1}^{N} \sum_{j=1}^{M_i} \hat{S}_{i,j}}{\sum_{i=1}^{N} M_i S_i} \tag{3.9}$$

This is computed over N images where M_i denotes the number of human-created segmentations of image i in the dataset. S_i is the number of segments the algorithm produced on image i, while $\hat{S}_{i,j}$

Medial Feature Superpixel	0.88
Ren et al. [128]	0.86
Felzenszwalb et al. [47]	0.83
Watershed on Distance Transform	0.79

Table 3.1. Performance of the algorithms.

is the number of segments produced by the superpixel algorithm that lie inside only one segment, j, of the human-created segmentation of image i. To compensate for some noise and uncertainty in the human segmentations, the criterion for $\hat{S}_{i,j}$ was relaxed such that only 95% of a superpixel had to be consistent with the human segmentation.

$\hat{S}_{i,j}$ is the number of superpixels that do not cross human segmentation boundaries

Intuitively, this performance measure represents the percentage of segments that do not cross a border of the segmentations drawn by the humans, normalized against the number of segments produced by the oversegmentation algorithm. Taking the mean of these values across all test images and all human segmentations for each of the images results in the performances reported in Table 3.1.

The performance measure favors low number of superpixels that do not cross object boundaries

All three algorithms possess free parameters that influence the properties and number of created superpixels (e.g. parameter k from [128] or the threshold θ for the seeding in our algorithm). These parameters were optimized by a grid search for the maximum of the performance measure using the training images of the Berkeley Segmentation Dataset. As a baseline method, we employed a standard watershed algorithm applied to the distance transformation of a Canny edge image.

Free parameters were optimized on the training set

The results of this performance measure indicate that the proposed medial feature segmentation yields better results than the other algorithms and is superior to the baseline method. Other performance measures (such as conservation of human segmentation boundaries) are also possible and might yield different results.

Our superpixels outperform state-of-the-art algorithms

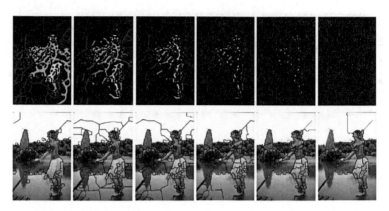

Figure 3.9. Influence of the threshold parameter θ for the seeding on the resulting superpixel segmentations. From left to right, the parameter is set to (0.2, 0.4, 0.6, 0.8, 1.1, 1.4). Top: $\mathcal{F} > \theta$, Bottom: Resulting oversegmentation.

However, we feel that the measure chosen here is appropriate since it provides an indicator for how useful the created superpixels will be for algorithms operating on them.

Optimal superpixels are smooth and do not require the user to specify the number of segments a-priori

The superior performance of our algorithm as compared to the competitors has several reasons: The algorithm by Felzenszwalb and Huttenlocher creates relatively ragged borders, which can be suboptimal for this performance measure. The superpixel algorithm based on normalized graph cuts produces smooth segment boundaries but as it produces a fixed number of segments (the number of superpixels k was optimized using the training data set), it cannot be optimal for a heterogeneous image set such as the Berkeley Segmentation dataset.

The threshold parameter θ influences the number of generated superpixels

As shown in Figure 3.10, the average number of superpixels generated by our algorithm depends on the threshold parameter θ. For large values of θ, only few distinct symmetry points are above the threshold and remain as seeds resulting in a small number of large segments. As the threshold becomes smaller, more seeds

68

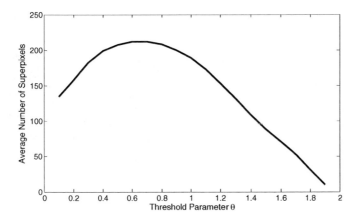

Figure 3.10. Influence of the thresholding parameter θ on the number of generated superpixels (averaged over all images in the Berkeley Segmentation Dataset).

are generated resulting in a higher number of starting areas for the watershed algorithm and consequently in a finer superpixel segmentation. However, the seed regions begin to merge for small values of θ as seen in the leftmost image of Figure 3.10, resulting in a lower number of segments. The location of the maximum depends on the properties of the underlying image.

The average runtime of the medial feature oversegmentation per image is 2.6 seconds in the current Matlab/C-Mex implementation, which is about as fast as the segmentation algorithm proposed by Felzenszwalb and Huttenlocher and much faster than the oversegmentation based on normalized graph cuts. However, the largest portion of this time is taken up by the iterative computation of the GVF field.

Average runtime is 2.6 seconds

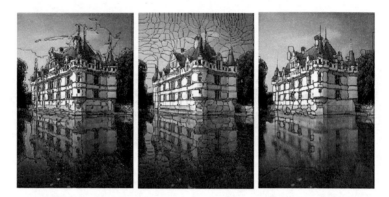

Figure 3.11. Results of different segmentation algorithms. **Left:** Segmentation obtained by superpixel algorithm after [47], which produces rather ragged boundaries. **Center:** The segmentation obtained by superpixel algorithm after [128] yields a fixed number of segments, which is too high in this case resulting in a highly segmented sky. **Right:** The oversegmentation result of our approach generates smooth regions and adapts the number of segments to the image structure (the sky is encoded by just one superpixel). Image taken from the Berkeley Segmentation Dataset [100].

3.2.4 Conclusion and Outlook

In this Section, we presented a novel way of image oversegmentation based on medial features. The medial features are computed by applying a divergence operator to the GVF field and are formed at points of high symmetry and are therefore well suited as seeds for a segmentation approach based on the watershed algorithm. Using such medial features allows our algorithm to be very efficient and offers many desirable properties such as stability against noise. We compared our algorithm to two state-of-the-art algorithms on the Berkeley Segmentation dataset. We showed that our method can serve as a basis for higher-level algorithms by producing a high percentage of segments that are consistent with segments found by human observers.

Future lines of investigation could include testing the performance of these superpixels in the context of human-centered applications, one of which is introduced in the next Chapter. This would allow an adaptation of the algorithm to meet the requirements of the user. Furthermore, extending the superpixel scheme to video data could provide a useful and compact 3-D representation of image sequences.

Another field of research is based on image reconstruction. Figure 3.12 shows reconstructions of several images from the Berkeley Segmentation Dataset. These were obtained by first extracting the superpixels according to the algorithm described above, and then rendering the superpixels back onto a canvas with the average color of all pixels in that superpixel. Apart from a pleasant visual effect, the reconstructed images show how most of the relevant information of the image is still kept even if the image is encoded by only a few superpixels and their mean colors.

Figure 3.12. Reconstruction of images based on superpixels. Each superpixel is rendered back onto a canvas with its mean color. The resulting mosaic-effect is not only visually pleasing but also retains most of the semantic information. Images taken from the Berkeley Segmentation Dataset [100]

Applications

*In the end we retain from our studies only that which
we practically apply.*

Johann Wolfgang von Goethe

In this Chapter, the application layer of this thesis will be discussed. The shape-centered features and representations described in the previous Chapters allow us to encode the content of an image in an efficient and compact manner. The evaluations in the previous Chapters have demonstrated the properties of the medial features when compared to other state-of-the-art features. However, another, less direct but possibly more convincing way of evaluating such schemes is by testing them in the context of real applications. To this end and to complete the arc from low-level features to high-level applications, the following Sections present three applications based on our shape-centered representations.

First, Section 4.1 presents a multi-class scene labeling framework based on medial feature representations. The goal of this application is to produce a dense semantic annotation of a whole

Applications allow us to evaluate the performance of the system with respect to a human observer

73

image to which end we combine a local prediction step based on medial feature superpixels with a global optimization scheme that employs conditional random fields (CRFs [78, 102, 87]. Section 4.2 presents a novel image retrieval technique based on semantic encodings of images. Finally, Section 4.3 presents a novel application in a driver-assistance context, where we learn to predict the likelihood that a pedestrian will be seen or missed by an observer.

4.1 Multi-Class Scene Labeling

Scene labeling aims at producing a dense semantic annotation of an entire image

Scene labeling is the logical extension to the traditional computer vision task of object recognition. Instead of finding and recognizing one object in an image the goal of scene labeling is, to take an image of a scene and label every entity in it simultaneously. This approach has the advantage of yielding dense semantic information, which in turn could be exploited by a wide variety of applications (e.g. the image retrieval task described in Section 4.2). Furthermore, scene labeling allows us to leverage the context in which entities occur in an image (e.g. cars are mostly found above the road and below the sky, the legs of a person are mostly located below the persons torso, etc.). The drawback is that scene labeling is a much more complicated task than visual object recognition or visual object classification. Natural images can contain a wide variety of different objects in a multitude of configurations and lighting conditions. The LabelMe database [133] is a good example of this problem. It consists of 182,637 images of which 58,137 contain human annotations (as of June 2010) of at least one object in the image. Via an interface, users can freely label the objects and consequently, LabelMe contains tens of thousands of different tags and object labels. This high number of object classes is partly due to the problem that 'classes' are not properly defined (as discussed by e.g. Malisiewicz [95]) but also because users are

74

allowed to name them freely, producing several synonyms for the same object (a dog can be labeled as 'dog', 'canine', 'animal', 'doggie', etc.).

Training thousands of object classifiers for the different classes is impractical and would lead to very poor results. Also, the difference between certain classes (e.g. 'bed' and 'couch') can be purely contextual or defined by other properties besides their visual appearance (c.f. the concept of affordances [53, 54]) making it impossible to train vision-based classifiers. Rosch et al. [130] introduced the concept of basic level categories (the highest level category that can be represented by one mental image), which make up our world. There are thousands of such categories for which classifiers would have to be trained to achieve human-level scene labeling. Obtaining enough training samples for all classes would pose a serious problem, but furthermore, even a very small 'false alarm' rate would lead to bad results in the final in multi-class recognition framework.

Defining a set of all possible object categories is a difficult and ambiguous task

We approach scene labeling from a different angle. We do not aim to label all possible classes in all possible images but only focus on a few ecological relevant categories in a constrained dataset. This allows us to build a well functioning system that can be useful in relevant situations while circumventing the problems inherent to multi-class scene labeling. Here, we operate on images depicting street scenes taken from the StreetScenes database [14] complying with all our demands (some examples from the database are shown in Figure 4.1). However, the same techniques described here could be applied to other sets of images and categories. The database is ecologically valid as it consists of natural images taken at eye-level by a human observer and it can provide useful insights into relevant situations e.g. driver assistance systems or navigation tasks. It contains human-made scene annotations for all images which we will consider as the ground-truth. Furthermore, it has only a

Our goal is to predict the labels for a few high-level categories in the StreetScenes database

75

Figure 4.1. Sample images from the MIT Street Scenes database[14].

limited set of labels (pedestrian, car, bicycle, building, tree, street, sidewalk and sky) thus restricting the intractable problem of classifying thousands of classes to a manageable problem with just eight 'super-classes'.

Albeit, the StreetScenes database has some drawbacks. The annotations in the database consists only of polygons (not of pixelwise bitmasks) and are consequently imprecise at the edges. Furthermore, in several cases there are missing or wrong labels (e.g. street labeled as pedestrians) and overlapping labels (e.g. groups of pixels labeled as street, car and pedestrian at the same time). Lastly, depending on the intended application scenario the limitation to eight classes can also be seen as a drawback. Examples of such faulty annotations in the StreetScenes database are depicted in Figure 4.2. These limitations imply that we face a situation where we can not fully trust the ground truth data and have to design the algorithms to be robust against wrong labels in the dataset. Another consequence arising from the imperfect labeling is that even a system performing optimally cannot reach 100% performance.

> The StreetScenes database contains some imperfect annotations which implies that optimal performance is not 100% accuracy

In the following Section 4.1.1, the state-of-the-art in scene labeling will be discussed. Afterwards, in Section 4.1.2 two approaches to multi-class scene labeling will be introduced. Section 4.1.3 details an evaluation of our labeling performance. Finally, Section 4.1.4 presents some conclusions and an outlook.

4.1.1 State-of-the-Art

Most approaches to segmentation deal with the problem of finding and labeling all pixels that belong to one object of interest known to be in the image. Among these methods the most important and successful ones are based on the watershed algorithm (e.g. [114]), on normalized cuts (e.g. [139]) and the implicit shape model [81], simultaneously dealing with object detection. A slightly differ-

> Most techniques focus on segmenting a single foreground object

Figure 4.2. Images from the MIT Street Scenes database [14] with problematic or faulty annotations. **Left:** Prominent objects in the image are not labeled at all ('car' is missing). **Center:** Only part of the image is labeled ('trees' in dark red and 'street' in yellow) the rest is not annotated (dark blue). **Right:** Some pixels in the overlap between the person and the car are labeled with three labels ('person', 'car' and 'street') and an algorithm has no way to determine the topmost one.

ent approach are interactive segmentation schemes (e.g. GrabCut [131]) that allow the user to mark the object of interest with a bounding box or few simple strokes. The algorithm expands the segmentation to engulf the whole object. These methods, however, aim at segmenting just a single object in the image and do not provide labels and segmentations for the whole image.

Current algorithms can predict the 3D geometry and surface orientation

Recently, algorithms have been proposed that are able to predict the orientation and some general properties for all pixels in the image. Saxena et al. [134] and Hoiem et al. [65, 67] follow such a scheme to predict the geometric structure and depth from a single still image, thus allowing them to reconstruct the associated 3-D geometry and manipulate the viewpoint of the image. However, these approaches neglect object knowledge and simply rely on learned low level image statistics and consequently do not create semantic labels.

78

A different line of recent research directly addressed the problem of assigning a high-level semantic label to each pixel in an image. Bileschi [13] used biologically motivated features to predict a dense labeling on the images from the StreetScenes database. Most closely related to our approach, is the work of Plath et al. [120] and He et al. [62], who also aimed at segmenting all objects in the scene simultaneously using context information provided by conditional random fields. However, their focus was mainly on the global optimization of the segmentation rather than the local prediction of labels.

Semantic scene labeling algorithms focus mainly on the global optimization

4.1.2 Optimizing Multi-Class Scene Labels

In this Section, we present our approach to achieve globally optimal multi-class scene labeling. We formalize the problem as an n-class classification problem where we aim to optimally select the label of each pixel in a test image from a set of n possible labels:

$$f : I \to L, \quad I \in \mathbb{R}^3, L \in [1 \dots n]^2, \tag{4.1}$$

where f is our labeling algorithm predicting a label $L(x, y)$ for each pixel in the image I. I and L have the same size. The idea is to approach the task by first classifying parts of the image locally (in our case superpixels) and then, based on those local estimates, find an optimal global solution, which ensures that certain contextual constraints are met. We follow two paths for the local classification. One based directly on the superpixels described in Section 3.2 and one based on the SIFT feature grouping from Section 3.1.

Our approach combines local prediction with global optimization

Local Prediction of Class Labels

We extract our superpixels from Section 3.2 along with a wide array of features for each one on each image

Our first approach is to segment each image into superpixels as described in Section 3.2.2, extract a wide array of features for each superpixel and then train a classifier to recognize the class memberships. It is vital to operate on superpixels instead of the pixel values themselves. As mentioned earlier, pixels are artifacts of the imaging process and do not correspond to valid entities in the world. Furthermore, the possibility to describe a pixel (apart from using its neighborhood) is limited to encoding the color and position, both of which do not necessarily correlate strongly with the class of the pixel. Our superpixels may still not represent entities in the world but they cluster together regions that are to some degree visually homogeneous and are therefore very likely to belong to the same (and furthermore only one) physical object. Superpixels also have the advantage that they have a larger spacial extend than normal pixels allowing us to extract a variety of features for each. Lastly, by clustering together visually similar pixels, superpixels allow us to classify large groups of pixels concurrently. As was shown in Section 3.2.3 our medial feature superpixels yield, to some extend, the optimal trade-off between pooling pixels into larger, more meaningful entities without merging pixels that should receive different class labels. We extracted a wide variety of features for each superpixel on the images from the StreetScenes database (for a complete list of features with description see Table 4.1).

The ratio of pixels to superpixels is class-dependent, which has to be accounted for by the loss function

Using the features from Table 4.1 we created a dataset of 800 training and 200 test samples on which we trained our multi-class classifier (the small sample size is chosen deliberately to make the model selection process computationally more feasible). Our final objective was to classify as many pixels as possible correctly, not as many superpixels as possible. Those two numbers are strongly

80

Name	# Dim	Description
Pos	2	Center of gravity of the superpixel [pixel]
Std	2	Standard deviation of the superpixel [pixel]
Area	1	Area of the superpixel [pixel]
HullInd	1	Number of corners comprising the convex hull of the superpixel
AreaPerHull	1	Area divided by the number of corners in the convex hull of the superpixel
MeanRGB	3	Mean color of the superpixel in RGB colorspace
MeanYCC	3	Mean color of the superpixel in YCC colorspace
StdRGB	3	Standard deviation of the color of the superpixel in RGB colorspace
StdYCC	3	Standard deviation of the color of the superpixel in YCC colorspace
IntHist	30	Histogram of intensity values of the pixels in the superpixel binned in 30 bins distributed equally through all 255 intensity levels
RGBHist	30	Histogram of RGB values of the pixels in the superpixel. Each color channel is binned into 10 equidistant bins
Texture	12	Texture descriptor representing the texture distribution for Gabor filter results of the superpixel at three different frequencies in four different orientations
TexStd	12	Texture roughness describing the standard deviation of the Texture descriptor throughout the superpixel

Table 4.1. Features used for the superpixel classification. The first column denotes the name of the feature, the second one its dimensionality and the third one provides a short description.

Class	#Pixels $(\times 10^9)$	# Superpixels $(\times 10^7)$
Pedestrian	0.02	0.02
Car	0.36	0.24
Bicycle	0.005	0.007
Building	1.28	1.06
Road	1.33	0.21
Sky	0.23	0.06
Sidewalk	0.34	0.13
Trees	0.51	0.56

Table 4.2. Number of pixels and superpixels summed over all images from the StreetScenes database. For certain classes the relative frequencies differ greatly. For the scene labeling task, it is best to adapt the training dataset (and consequently the empirical risk) to the frequencies of the pixels as this is closer to the true loss.

correlated for most classes but differ strongly for other classes as seen in Table 4.2. Taking equal numbers of superpixels from all classes would over-represent classes such as 'bicycle' in the loss function, which are rare in the images. We cannot adapt the number of superpixels in the training set to match their frequencies in the StreetScene images neither, because this would lead to large numbers of superpixels from the highly textured classes such as 'trees', producing a huge number of small superpixels. To address these issues, we created our database by randomly sampling super-pixels from the StreetScenes database according to the number of pixels that are labeled for each class for all classes (see Table 4.2). As mentioned earlier, some of the superpixels have multiple labels (e.g. segments labeled as 'car', 'pedestrian' and 'street' simultane-ously in Figure 4.2). To prevent ambiguities in our training set, we only took superpixels that have only one label.

SVMs are employed as local classifiers

Based on this dataset, we trained a multi-class classifier that will be able to predict the labels of novel test superpixels. This is a difficult task and requires a robust classifier. We chose the

Support Vector Machine (SVM, c.f. [25, 153]) with an RBF kernel as classifier, which has proved to produce state-of-the-art results even on small and noisy datasets. We employed the freely available libsvm [24] implementation to train and test our SVMs. For a more detailed introduction to support vector machines, see e.g. Schölkopf et al. [137].

The total dimensionality of all combined features is 93. We normalized the feature vectors to ensure that each dimension has a mean of zero and a standard deviation of one (variance normalization). This is a standard procedure in machine learning to guarantee that no single dimension will dominate the ensuing distance calculations in feature space. Without normalization, distance judgments between two feature vectors could be dominated by one dimension, whose variance is e.g. a couple of magnitudes larger than the rest. As the number of feature dimensions is high when compared to the number of training samples we run into the so-called *curse of dimensionality* (see [8, 9, 12]). This observation states that as the dimensionality of a problem increases the number of samples that is needed to evenly fill the space grows exponentially. A classical example is that 100 samples suffice to sample the space between zero and one evenly in 0.01 intervals in 1-D while it needs 10^{20} to achieve the same sampling in 10-D. The implication of this observation is that distance measures become increasingly meaningless in higher dimensions. Furthermore, we can assume that there is a certain amount of redundancy between dimensions (especially between the different color histograms). To combat this problem, we performed dimensionality reduction via principle components analysis (PCA). This did not improve the performance significantly, most likely because some of the features have lots of dimensions which contain noise. In such scenarios, linear dimension reduction techniques such as PCA do not yield good results. Consequently, a feature selection technique (for more in-

The high dimensionality of the feature vector implies that we have to do feature selection to circumvent the curse of dimensionality

Linear dimension reduction with PCA does not yield significant improvements

formation and references of feature selection techniques confer [68]) that picks an optimal subset of features for the regression task is needed. As the number of possible feature-combinations grows exponentially with the number of features, a search for the optimum by enumerating all combinations is infeasible. Therefore, we used a straight-forward heuristic to simultaneously select features and optimize the free parameters of the SVM (the regularization parameter C and the σ of the radial basis function (RBF) Kernel). We randomly initialized all parameters and the feature selection, trained the SVR on the training set and used the cross-validation error as a measure of the performance. We trained a large number of SVMs (in the order of 20.000) in this manner, while continuously updating and keeping the 100 ones. We checked the distribution of parameters and selection of features in the remaining 100 SVMs and narrowed the search space while making the search more fine grained. This method is closely related to *simulated annealing* [76] methods and yields a result that is very likely to be close to the optimum. Since this problem is easily parallelizable, as training one SVM is independent of the others, computation time is not a critical issue. Table 4.3 shows, which features were finally selected by our heuristic.

A second approach to the local classification problem is based on the corner-grouping from Section 3.1

Apart from this approach, which is based on superpixel classification, we also tested a second local labeling scheme based on the classification of grouped SIFTs as introduced in Section 3.1. Using our framework we can extract shape-centered and corner-based interest points, group them together using the gradient vector flow fields and classify the shape-centered interest points based on the graph of the connected SIFT descriptors using kNN (described already in Section 3.1.2). We adapted the frequencies of the SCIPs for each class in the training dataset in the same way as we did with the superpixels by using the pixel frequencies shown in Table 4.2. One issue with this approach is that it will only provide labels

84

Name	# Dim
Pos	2
Std	2
MeanRGB	3
HullInd	1
MeanYCC	3
RGBHist	30
Texture	12

Table 4.3. The entries that were selected by our feature selection algorithm. It is difficult to interpret these results because of the non-linear nature of SVMs but it can be noted that the dimensionality has been reduced drastically and the selected features seem to be less redundant as the full feature set.

at sparse locations (namely at the interest points). Consequently, we needed a mechanism, which expands the sparse labeling to the whole image. To fill the gaps between the interest points, we again employed our superpixels from Section 3.2.2. There can be more than one SCIP inside a single superpixel, which means that we need a way to combine the predictions yielded by the interest points in a given segment. Since, we used a SVM that predicts probabilities for all possible class labels we can achieve the combination by pointwise multiplication of the different probability distributions over the possible classes. For this to be correct, we have to assume that the random variables (the predicted labels for each SCIP) are independent. Although, this assumption is violated, because SCIPs that are located in the same superpixel are likely to share several connected interest points, we still obtained good results.

Global Optimization of the Annotation

A global optimization step introduces contextual constraints and smoothes the annotation

The previous Section discussed how we can predict the labels of superpixels locally. This does not take into account the context of the superpixels and certain smoothness constraints that occur in natural images. Figure 4.3 shows an example of the labels as they were predicted by the classifier. The quality is already good but there is room for improvement, where the prediction can benefit from a global optimization step. For example, the windows in the building that have erroneously been classified as sky are surrounded by superpixels that have correctly been detected as 'building'. When looking through the database of training images such a hypothesis can easily be discarded for the more plausible one that the windows actually belong to the building as well.

Figure 4.3. **Left:** An image from the StreetScenes database and the overlayed superpixel boundaries (red). **Right:** The labels predicted by the local prediction step of our framework. The windows of the building are labeled as 'sky' but are surrounded by 'building' superpixels. This is an example of an error that can be easily compensated by a global optimization scheme.

Conditional Random Fields (CRF) are discriminative probabilistic models

To obtain a globally valid hypothesis in a meaningful way, we have to learn contextual dependencies of the labels from the data. To this end we employ discriminative probabilistic model called Conditional Random Fields (CRF) [78, 102, 87]. In the following

86

paragraphs, we first present a quick general overview introducing the main concept of CRFs following to some degree the nomenclature of [156] and then present the application of CRFs to the problem of multi-class scene labeling.

The objective for CRFs is to learn a probabilistic model given a set of observations $\mathbf{X}$ and a set of associated labels $\mathbf{Y}$. A CRF then models the conditional probability distribution $p(\mathbf{Y}|\mathbf{X})$, which is the major difference to Hidden Markov Models (HMM, for an introduction to HMMs e.g. [124]), which model the joint probability distribution $p(\mathbf{X}, \mathbf{Y})$ of the data. After learning, the CRF avails the possibility to do inference with it and predict the optimal label y^* for a set of observations x^*. The CRF can be thought of as an undirected graphical model $G(V, E)$ with nodes $v \in V$ representing the random variables from $\mathbf{X}$ and $\mathbf{Y}$ and the edges $e \in E$ encoding the conditional dependencies and independences in the model. The structure of the graphical model G depends on the data and has to be modeled by the user. The simplest case is a linear chain as shown in Figure 4.4.

CRFs model the conditional density $p(\mathbf{Y}|\mathbf{X})$

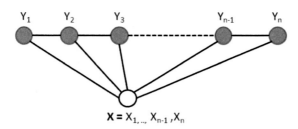

Figure 4.4. A graphical model of a linear chain CRF. The shaded variables Y_i are the unobserved labels, which can depend on all observed variables $\mathbf{X}$.

The labels $\mathbf{Y}$ in the model are globally conditioned on the observations $\mathbf{X}$ meaning that in contrast to HMMs all observations can influence each label $y_i \in \mathbf{Y}$. This implies that CRFs do not

The labels are globally conditioned on the observations

87

have to make independence assumptions about the observations, which is a drawback of HMMs. The independences between the labels **Y** are defined by the structure of the graph. As demonstrated by Lafferty et al. [78], the Hammersley-Clifford theorem [59] is applicable here meaning that the probability distribution can be restated as a normalized product of potential functions defined over the maximal cliques of the graph. Following this, in the case of the linear chain from Figure 4.4, we obtain potential function of the form:

$$exp(\sum_j \lambda_j t_j(y_{i-1}, y_i, \mathbf{x}, i) + \sum_k \mu_k s_k(y_i, \mathbf{X}, i)), \qquad (4.2)$$

$p(\mathbf{Y}|\mathbf{X})$ can be rewritten as a product of *unary* and *pairwise* potentials

where $t_j(y_{i-1}, y_i, \mathbf{x}, i)$ is a function defining the pairwise potential between two adjacent label nodes y_{i-1} and y_i given an observation $\mathbf{x}$ at position i in the chain. $s_k(y_i, \mathbf{X}, i)$ is the observation function (called 'unary potential') that defines the matching between the label y_i and the observation $\mathbf{X}$. λ_j and μ_k are parameters that have to be estimated from the training data. A more intuitive explanation is that t is a function that describes how well a clique (in the case of a chain two adjacent label nodes) fit together (in case of an image, how likely it is to have superpixel with the label 'cat' next to superpixel labeled as 'space shuttle'). The potential s describes how well the label is supported by the data (e.g. how likely it is that a superpixel that is mainly green should carry the label 'face').

The potentials can be expressed as linear combinations of feature functions

Defining the potential function would theoretically be very hard as one would have to fit them to the complex probability distributions. In practice, this problem is avoided by expressing the potential functions in terms of features $b(\mathbf{x}, i)$ that describe some property of the observations $\mathbf{X}$ like 'Is the brightness of the pixel above 200?'. Based on these features, the learning algorithm can optimize λ_j and μ_k such that the resulting probability distribution closely matches the empirical distribution of the training samples. We can generalize the two potential functions s and t to:

$$F_j(\mathbf{y}, \mathbf{x}) = \sum_{i=1}^{n} f_j(y_{i-1}, y_i, \mathbf{x}, i), \qquad (4.3)$$

where $f_j(y_{i-1}, y_i, \mathbf{x}, i)$ is one of the two potential functions $t_j(y_{i-1}, y_i, \mathbf{x}, i)$ and $s_k(y_i, \mathbf{X}, i)$ as expressed by feature functions $b(\mathbf{x}, i)$. Because of the Hammersley theorem we can now factorize the probability distribution into potentials:

$$p(\mathbf{y}|\mathbf{x}, \lambda) = \frac{1}{Z(\mathbf{x})} exp \left(\sum_j \lambda_j F_j(\mathbf{y}, \mathbf{x}) \right) \qquad (4.4)$$

Since the potential can still be any real valued positive functions, we have to normalize the equation by dividing through $Z(\mathbf{x})$ to ensure that the result is a valid probability. For a more detailed introduction to conditional random fields refer to [78, 156].

Here, we explain how we adapted the idea of CRFs to our special case of globally optimizing the scene labeling. First, we have to define a graph structure $G(V, E)$, which emerges naturally from the superpixel segmentation. Each superpixel is represented by a node $v \in V$ and is connected by an undirected edge $e \in E$ with all nodes representing adjacent superpixels with which it shares a border (see Figure 4.5). Since, the length of the shared border can be a weak indicator of the connection strength, we define the accumulated flux flow $\mathcal{F}$ along the border as weight for each edge (see Figure 4.6). Between two superpixels that lie on the same shape the border will be comprised of low values of F yielding a strong indication that the labels for both superpixels should be the same. For superpixels that lie on either side of a salient edge in the image, $\mathcal{F}$ will be rather high and we can subsequently reduce the penalty for different labelings in such cases (see Figure 4.6).

The adjacency of the superpixels yields the graphical model $G(V, E)$ with an edge strength determined by $\mathcal{F}$

Figure 4.5. The graph structure $G(V, E)$ is determined by the adjacency of the superpixels. **Left:** Original image. **Center:** Overlayed superpixel boundaries (green). **Right:** The center superpixel node is connected to all adjacent nodes via edges (red). The strength of the edges is determined by $\mathcal{F}$ as shown in Figure 4.6. Image taken from the Caltech 101 database [45, 46].

Figure 4.6. The connection strength between two adjacent superpixels is closely related to the accumulated flux flow along their shared border (center image). Superpixels that have a strongly negative flux flow along their border are separated by a salient edge and probably belong to different shapes (red arrows in the right image). Images with a non-negative flux flow along the border probably belong to the same shape (green arrows in the right image). Image taken from the Caltech 101 database [45, 46].

The local predictors yield a probability distribution over all possible class labels for each superpixel: $p(\mathbf{c}|SP)$, where $\mathbf{c}$ is a random variable over all classes and SP is the descriptor of the current superpixel. Based on this probability distribution, we define the unary potential that measures how well the label y_i matches the features X as $\phi_{\text{unary}} = p(y_i|\mathbf{c})$. Learning ϕ_{unary} would be difficult because $\mathbf{c}$ is a probability distribution. Hence, we approximate it by substituting $\mathbf{c}$ with c_w the label with the highest probability. This can be learned from training data by straightforward counting and normalization. We define the pairwise potential $\phi_{pairwise}(y_i, y_j)$ that represents how probable it is to find the labels y_i and y_j in adjacent superpixels. This can also be learned from training data by counting and subsequent normalization.

The potential functions can be learned from the training data

With the graph structure and the two potential functions, we have defined the properties of our CRF on which we can do inference. To this end, we need a solver that computes the optimal set of labels $\mathbf{y}$ for the whole image for a given instance of features. We use the GCMex solver by Veksler et al. [18, 51], which computes GraphCuts (first introduced in computer vision by Greig et al. [58]) to solve the inference problem on a CRF. For this particular solver we had to restate the potentials as cost functions:

The Graph Cuts algorithm is used to do inference in the CRF

$$C_{unary} = \alpha_1 * (1 - \phi_{unary}), \qquad (4.5)$$

$$C_{pairwise} = \alpha_2 * (1 - \phi_{pairwise}), \qquad (4.6)$$

where the α's are parameters that have to be learned from the training data. In our case, the learning is done by a grid-search over a wide array of α's. We initialize $\mathbf{y}$ with the most probable labels c_w.

In this Section, we have discussed how the local prediction and the global optimization of the scene labeling is performed. It would be more correct to optimize the classification and the global optimization using the CRF simultaneously. However, this would make the task intractable with respect to computation power and number of free parameters.

4.1.3 Evaluation

For the evaluation the classes in the StreetScenes database were combined into five 'super-classes'

We evaluate our system on a subset of 1000 randomly drawn and previously unseen (by our algorithm) images from the StreetScenes database. To simplify the evaluation, we combined the classes 'street' and 'sidewalk' to one 'street' class, because the two classes differ only slightly in their visual appearance and their main differences are contextual. Furthermore, we combined the three foreground classes 'pedestrian', 'car' and 'bicycle' into one 'foreground' class. This has been done to avoid heavily unbalanced classes during the training since the foreground classes all had significantly fewer examples than the background classes. Moreover, just knowing the locations of possible foreground objects is already sufficient for most computer vision tasks and the true class of the found 'object' can then be determined by a subsequent, specialized classifier. This resulted in a five-class scene labeling problem that we used for evaluation purposes. The five classes are: 'foreground', 'street', 'building', 'tree' and 'sky'.

'Portion of correctly predicted pixels in the test images' is used as performance measure

First, we tested the performance of our two local classification strategies (based on superpixels and on grouped features). We extracted our superpixels (discussed in Section 3.2) from all images in the test data set. On average, there were 1504 superpixels per image. We obtained the ground truth labels of the superpixel by extracting all labeled pixels associated with the current superpixel region from the human annotations. This can lead to situations in which a superpixel has several labels associated with it, either because it crosses a border between two objects or because some pixels are annotated with multiple labels (c.f. the examples with suboptimal labelings in Figure 4.2). As we cannot determine a

92

Class	Superpixel (portion correct)	Grouped Sift (portion correct)
Foreground	0.32	0.33
Street	0.92	0.57
Building	0.56	0.29
Foliage	0.74	0.65
Sky	0.60	0.36

Table 4.4. Performance of the local prediction step using the superpixel and the grouped SIFT feature method in portion correct. Values indicate the percentage of correctly predicted pixels in the image.

single correct label for such superpixels, we accepted any of the labels found in the superpixel as correct. Furthermore, there are superpixels, with no labeled pixels associated with them, again due to imperfect labeling (e.g. Figure 4.2 (center)). We removed these from the test dataset. The average performance of the two multi-class labeling schemes is listed in Table 4.4. As performance measure, we chose the portion of pixels (not superpixels) that were correctly classified for each class. Some examples of the local classification are shown in Figure 4.7.

As we can see, the local classification based on the superpixels outperformed the classification performance based on the grouped SIFTs for all classes (except the foreground class for which both methods perform equally well). This is probably because SIFTs are best suited for object detection and optimized for the foreground classes, whereas this task deals mainly with the background classes. The classes in the database can be well described by information about their color, structure and position, all of which are not available to the grouped-SIFT classifier.

Next, we evaluated the global optimization based on the local predictions. To this end, we took the prediction of the superpixel classifiers and used the graph cut optimization framework based on

Superpixel classification is better adapted to predict the classes in our dataset

Performance has greatly increased after global optimization

93

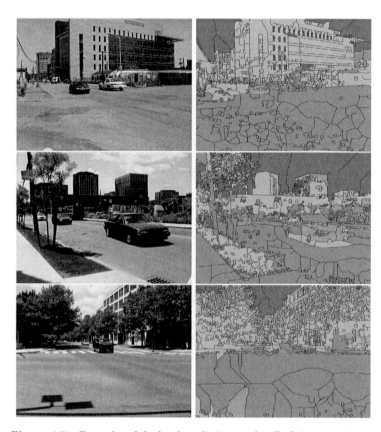

Figure 4.7. Examples of the local prediction results. Each image pair represents an image from the StreetScenes database and the corresponding local multi-class predictions. Colors indicate predicted class (blue=sky, gray=street, brown=building, green=foliage, orange=foreground object). Images taken from the MIT Street Scenes database [14].

Class	Superpixel (portion correct)	after optimization (portion correct)
Foreground	0.32	0.38
Street	0.92	0.94
Building	0.56	0.71
Foliage	0.74	0.86
Sky	0.60	0.72

Table 4.5. Performance increase from the local prediction to the global optimization step in portion correct. Values indicate the portion of correctly predicted pixels in the image.

the trained CRF model to obtain a globally valid and smoothed image annotation. Table 4.5 details the results and Figure 4.8 shows examples of the resulting annotations.

The performance has increased significantly by the global optimization scheme. However, the results are still not perfect. This might be due to the ambiguities in the database, which influences not only the validation performance but also making the training complex and noisy. The poor results for the 'foreground' class (32% before optimization and 38% afterwards, see Table 4.5) is probably due to our features, which are better suited to classify background objects.

This might already be close to theoretically optimal performance

4.1.4 Conclusion and Outlook

In this Section, we presented a multi-class scene labeling framework based on the mid-level, shape-centered image representations introduced in the previous Chapter. The approach combines a local prediction step, in which the semantic label of a single superpixel is estimated with a global optimization scheme, using CRFs to form a globally coherent annotation. The evaluation shows that most background classes can be predicted quite well and that the global

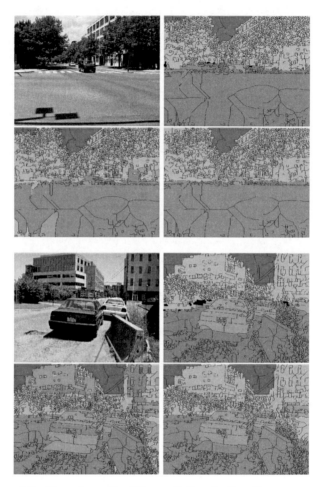

Figure 4.8. Example results of the prediction pipeline. Shown are sets of four images (the original (top left), the human annotation (top right), the local prediction (bottom left) and the result of the global optimization (bottom right). Colors indicate predicted class (blue=sky, gray=street, brown=building, green=foliage, orange=foreground object, black=missing entry). Images taken from the MIT Street Scenes database [14].

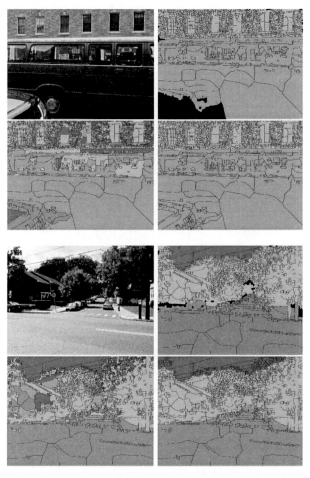

Figure 4.9. Example results of the prediction pipeline (cont.). Shown are sets of four images (the original (top left), the human annotation (top right), the local prediction (bottom left) and the result of the global optimization (bottom right).Colors indicate predicted class (blue=sky, gray=street, brown=building, green=foliage, orange=foreground object, black=missing entry)

optimization step yields a significant performance increase.

Future lines of investigation could include the combination of superpixels and grouped corner interest points and the introduction of higher level information such as scene gist. Furthermore, using the automatically generated annotation in an application with humans-in-the-loop could provide parameters and constraints about which classes have to be detected with which performance.

The presented scheme allows us to generate rough high-level semantic knowledge about given images automatically. This information can be used in several ways, for example by the image retrieval algorithm presented in the next Section.

4.2 Sketch Search

There are millions of image searches performed every day, which to date rely mainly on text-based queries. With the advent of increasingly powerful computer vision systems for object detection, segmentation (like the one presented in the previous Section) and tracking, and the introduction of large labeled image databases such as LabelMe [133], the possibility arises for more advanced image retrieval tools to exploit this additional information. Thus, image retrieval is an important application that links the output of computer vision algorithms to a human observer, allowing us to evaluate the performance of our methods not only in an algorithmic way but also with respect to the end-user. We introduce a novel image retrieval framework for finding images based on semantic sketches in large labeled databases.

Semantics can be a valuable source for image retrieval tools

Traditionally, Content-Based Image Retrieval (CBIR) systems rely primarily on image statistics and machine learning techniques to select matching images from a database. This might not be the optimal way to approach the problem as it neglects sources of high-level information, for instance image annotations. As the discipline of computer vision progresses, it is reasonable to expect a steep increase in the number and availability of labeled images.

Automatically generated image annotations can enhance CBIR systems

We propose a retrieval system that allows the user to formulate semantic queries intuitively rather than working with photometric queries. As opposed to many other sketch-based CBIR systems, we do not require the user to draw detailed sketches of the object classes. Our intuitive interface enables the user to indicate the semantic composition of the desired image with the help of semantic brushes (such as a brush for the classes 'car' or 'sky'). Since we operate on high-level information, searches can be performed very efficiently using a tree structure, in contrast to linear methods, which are infeasible in large-scale retrieval scenarios. Our

Our systems enables the user to search for images based on semantic compositions

Figure 4.10. Two example queries for street scene images and one for coastal images with top five matches. Colors in the query sketch denote semantic classes.

intended application is finding images that roughly match a user's wishes, not a target search for one specific image, which would require higher developed sketching abilities from the user.

A user study with the StreetScnenes database demonstrates the validity of our approach

To evaluate and validate our system, we performed a user study with 10 participants. They were asked to sketch street scenes and rate the images that were retrieved by our system. For the user study and most of the algorithmic evaluations, we used the StreetScenes database [14], which contains more than 3500 images with labels of eight classes (pedestrian, car, bicycle, street, sidewalk, building, sky and tree). This database provides a suitable testbed for our algorithm as it contains a large number of images from one type of scene category. It can be viewed as a dense sampling of a small part of image space akin to what would result from a computer vision algorithm that automatically labels a vast quantity of images.

The main contributions of our method include: the usage of high-level semantic sketches, its computational efficiency, which makes it applicable to large-scale image searches, its robustness, which leads to very low requirements on users sketching abilities, and its validity as demonstrated by a user study.

100

In Section 4.2.1, we describe previous work in this field and contrast the proposed framework to it. Section 4.2.2 describes the employed distance measures, the decision trees and the interface that comprises this system. Section 4.2.4 details the evaluation and the user study that have been performed to validate this method. Section 4.2.5 explains some of the limitations of image retrieval using semantic sketches. Finally, Section 4.2.6 provides a summary and an outlook toward future work.

4.2.1 State-of-the-Art

Image retrieval systems aim to return images that are consistent with the user's query. The need for such systems has motivated a large body of research literature. In the early studies of this research field, the user was asked to specify the query in terms of visual features such as color or texture, which was named Query By Image Content (QBIC) (cf. [49] or [70], which is the basis for the *Retrievr* system by *Flickr*). These queries were then compared with appearance models of images in the database. Another class of early approaches to CBIR required the user to provide an example image for the search. The following Query By Visual Example (QBVE) allowed the system to calculate more complex image correlation measures (e.g., [96, 63]). Both lines of approaches suffer from the so-called 'semantic gap' i.e., the lack of correspondence between visual and semantic features. They yield results that have the desired low-level properties (e.g., images of a black dog and a black car) but may not fulfill the user's semantic wishes (e.g., containing a black dog versus containing any black shape). For a concise review of earlier CBIR approaches and an extensive list of references, the reader is referred to [143].

One approach to bridge this 'semantic gap' is to use text-based queries, as offered by such image search services as *Google*, *Bing* or *Flickr*. These approaches employ semantics in form of key-

Classical image retrieval tools suffer from the semantic gap

101

Text-based queries do not allow the specification of desired spatial relationships in the image

words that are assigned to images, text surrounding images in web pages, as well as manually and automatically created annotations of objects, regions and scene classes. A vast amount of research is devoted to the question on how to create these labels in an unsupervised fashion (e.g., [6, 157]). These systems mostly rely on purely text-based searches, ignoring the wealth of information available in the image.

QBSE systems allow the user to specify semantic properties of the desired image, but are mostly not applicable to large-scale scenarios

Text-based systems do not allow the user to specify a concrete image composition she or he has in mind. This can be addressed by allowing the user to draw a query image using regions of photometric patches (e.g. [44]). The photometric patches are generated in an unsupervised fashion from training data. This can be seen as an example of a recent approach called Query By Semantic Example (QBSE). In systems such as [126, 125], the user specifies an image from which a computer vision system extracts semantic properties. These properties are subsequently compared to the images in the database to retrieve images that are semantically similar to the query image. Because of the difficult similarity judgments needed to find matches, such systems are often not applicable for real-time searches in large databases. Further reviews on semantical image retrieval can be found in [34, 90], a review on the usability of semantic search tools is the subject of [152]. Our algorithm falls roughly in this category of QBSE even though we allow users to freely draw a high-level composition rather than requiring them to provide an image similar to the one the user is looking for.

Photo synthesis can generate images with the desired semantic properties *de-novo* but requires advanced sketching abilities

A quite different approach to the problem of image retrieval is photo montage or photo synthesis, which aims to create the image the user has in mind instead of searching for an similar existing image in a database. The system described in [71] allows the user to specify semantic regions similar to our system. Based on this sketch, the system automatically retrieves image parts and stitches them together to form a coherent image. Sketch2Photo ([26]) also

102

lets the user specify objects at any position in the image, but requires her to sketch the objects themselves and annotate them with text labels. This gives the user the freedom to use any object label that an Internet image search can reasonably retrieve images for, and also allows finer control over the objects' appearance, but requires good sketching abilities and iterative refinement of the results.

For further references on image retrieval systems and their evaluation, confer [140, 154].

4.2.2 Image Retrieval Using Semantic Sketches

Our retrieval algorithm employs a tree structure similar to a random decision forest [64] to retrieve candidate matches from the database and a fine grained search through the returned matches to determine a ranking. This scheme allows it to perform very fast searches (on average 0.23 milliseconds per search in a tree containing one million images on a standard desktop PC) with a time complexity of $O(m \log n)$ where m is the number of trees and n the number of images (cf. Figure 4.18).

Our retrieval algorithm has the complexity of $O(m \log n)$

Matching-Cost Function

It is central for such a system to define a cost function $C(Q, I)$, which measures the quality of the match between a query sketch Q and an image I. This cost function allows the algorithm to rank the images and present a few top-ranking search results to the user. Desirable features of such a cost function are a high correlation between the returned matches and the image the user had in mind (which will be discussed in Section 4.2.4) and robustness against the bad drawing skills of the average user (see Section 4.2.4 and Figure 4.22).

$C(Q, I)$ measures the quality of the match between query and image

In our case, the queries Q are given as a set of N binary arrays

103

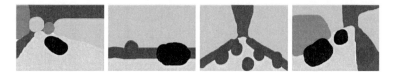

Figure 4.11. Some examples of queries in our semantic image retrieval scheme taken from the experiment. The colors relate to semantic object categories. (red=car, gray=street, dark gray=sidewalk, brown=building, blue=sky, green=foliage, dark blue=pedestrian)

We assume a rough binary annotation for all searchable classes in the images

Q_i of size [32x32], that denote the position in the image where objects of class i should be located, for each object class $i = 1 \ldots N$ (c.f. sample queries in Figure 4.11). We assume that for each image I in our database, we are given a set of binary annotations A_i that are *true* at the positions of objects of a class i and *false* everywhere else. This annotation only needs to be roughly correct as minor errors do not influence the performance of our algorithms. As demonstrated in the previous Section, obtaining such a rough annotation for several high level classes automatically is feasible.

The searchable representation requires 1kB per image and object class

For each image and each class, we compute distance transformations D_{Ti}, which denote the minimal distance of each pixels to the nearest occurrence of an object of class i in the image. To achieve invariance against scaling and to allow variable aspect ratios in the dataset, we rescale all annotations to [320x320] pixels before applying the distance transformation. In order to reduce the memory footprint of the resulting D_{Ti}, we scale them down to [32x32] pixels allowing us to represent annotations and queries with descriptors of 1024 bytes per object class.

A more robust distance transformation based on the GVF can help with noisy and probabilistic annotations

In the case of perfect human annotations, the standard distance transformation is sufficient. However, automatic annotation schemes can yield probabilistic or noisy annotations in which case a more robust distance measure is needed. We can define such a robust distance transformation similar to the idea of the traces for feature grouping in Section 3.1. For each annotation, we compute the normalized GVF field V_N for each class i. We initialize a trace $T_0(x, y)$ at each image location (x, y) and follow the vectors in V_N according to the following equation:

$$T_{n+1}(x, y) = T_n(x, y) + V_N(T_n(x, y))$$

Based on this we can count the number of iterations it takes for a trace $T_0(x, y)$ initialized at position (x, y) to reach the first *true* pixel of the annotation A_i of class i:

$$d_i(x, y) = \operatorname*{argmin}_{N} (A_i(T_N(x, y)) = 1) \tag{4.7}$$

This gives us a robust distance transformation $d_i(x, y)$ that can be precomputed for each image and each class. We have mentioned earlier that we interpret V_N as the gradient of the noise-free distance transformation. Thus, this scheme can be seen as integrating over this noise-free gradient of the distance transformation, yielding a noise-free distance transformation.

$d_i(x, y)$ is the noise-free distance transformation

Based on one of these two distance transformations (the standard distance transformation D_T and our robust distance $d_i(x, y)$ from Equation 4.7), we now define a straight-forward cost function that can be evaluated very quickly using the scalar product between query sketch and distance transformation summed up over all classes in the image and the sketch: $C(Q, I) = \sum_i^N \langle Q_i, D_{Ti} \rangle$. An intuitive interpretation of this scheme is that we accumulate the distance that each pixel set in the query image Q_i has to travel to the nearest pixel containing the queried object in the image. If the image I does not contain all objects that are present in the query Q, we add a high penalty κ to the cost function:

$C(Q, I)$ sums the distances each query pixel is away from the nearest *true* pixel in the annotation

105

$$C\left(Q, I\right) = \sum_{i}^{N} \langle Q_i, D_{Ti} \rangle + \kappa(Q, A)$$

$$\kappa(Q, A) = \left\{ \begin{array}{ll} 0 & \text{if all classes from } Q \text{ exist in } A \\ \text{const} & \text{otherwise} \end{array} \right.$$

$C\left(Q, I\right)$ can be augmented to accommodate additional search parameters such as color

A depiction of the evaluation of the cost function is shown in Figure 4.12. Using such an intuitively plausible cost function allows us to easily optimize and augment our system. Linear weighting of the different classes and adding additional cost terms to represent for example further query properties such as the color of the objects are straightforward augmentations to the cost function. Figure 4.13 shows how the results are reweighed when adding a cost term for color $C_{\text{col}}\left(Q_{\text{col}}, I\right)$. We implemented this cost term by computing the earth mover distance (EMD c.f. [132]) between the color Q_{col} the user has specified for each region (black regions denote regions where the user does not care about the color) and the normalized histogram of the region in the image where the object is present. The EMD provides a suitable distance measure between two color histograms and yields better results than for example comparing the mean colors of two regions:

$$C_{\text{col}}\left(Q_{\text{col}}, I\right) = \sum_{i}^{N} \text{EMD}\left(Q_{\text{col},i}, \text{hist}\left(A_i \times I\right)\right) .$$

The augmented cost function is:

$$C\left(Q, Q_{\text{col}}, I\right) = \sum_{i}^{N} \alpha_i \times \langle Q_i, D_{Ti} \rangle + C_{\text{col}}\left(Q_{\text{col}}, I\right) + \kappa .$$

At this point, the α's are set by hand. They cannot be optimized based solely on the database as the main evaluation criterion

106

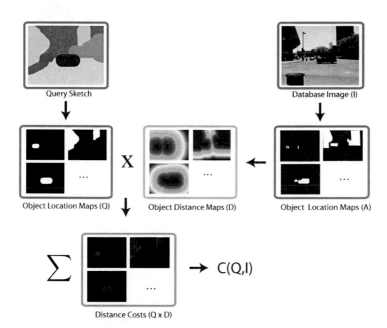

Figure 4.12. Pipeline for evaluating the matching cost between an image I and a query sketch Q: for each semantic class, a binary object location map is created. A distance transformation is applied. It yields a map that contains the distance from each pixel to the nearest pixel of an object. The query sketch is also translated into a set of object location maps, which are multiplied pixelwise with the distance maps. Summing over all pixels and classes results in the matching cost.

Figure 4.13. Constraining the image search: The top row shows a search for a car on a street in front of a building. The second row shows the results when searching for the same configuration with the additional constraint that the car should be white. The third row shows the same search, but now constraint to gray buildings. Result images are from the MIT Street Scenes database [14].

for such a system is how well the results match what the user had in mind. They have to be determined in larger user studies.

Decision Trees

Random decision forests make the approach applicable to large-scale scenarios

For small datasets containing only a few thousand images, the evaluation of the cost function for each image is feasible albeit time-consuming. As the size of the labeled dataset grows, a linear search becomes intractable, especially in the context of an envisioned webscale application. However, for most applications we do not need a full ranking of all images in the database, but only need to retrieve a couple of the top ranked images. We address this problem by using a heuristic inspired by random decision forests [64]. Since the similarity of two images in the database depends critically on the query (e.g. which image properties we are looking for), we cannot examine the similarities for each class separately but have to take the whole image into account at each decision node (cf. Figure 4.14).

108

Each random decision tree in our forest contains a pivot annotation $a \in A$ and a threshold σ at each inner node. At this node, the cost function $C(Q, I)$ for an incoming element is evaluated. If it is smaller than σ, it is forwarded to the left child and otherwise to the right child of the node. During creation of the trees, we select a random pivot element, calculate the costs to all images at that node and take the median of the costs as threshold σ. Taking the median guarantees that the resulting tree will be balanced and all searches can be performed in $O(\log n)$ time. We stop splitting the nodes when the number of elements at one node drops below a threshold (in our case, five images). Consequently, any search in a tree returns one to four candidate matches, but further matches can be retrieved by traversing the tree backwards (backtracking).

The depth of our trees is guaranteed to be $O(\log n)$

By evaluating the cost function with respect to a pivot element at each node, we achieve a data-driven partitioning of the image annotation space. Different pivot elements lead to different trees, which will highlight different aspects of the cost function. To make full use of this, we search through a forest containing m trees (usually 20). We obtain the final presentation order by ranking all returned results according to the cost function. Consequently, the total runtime of a search is $O(m \times \log n + m \times k)$ where k is the fixed time it takes to evaluate the cost function for the resulting matches returned by one tree.

Queries can be evaluated in logarithmic runtime

We show that the results returned by our forest approximate the matches returned by a linear search in Section 4.2.4. We further demonstrate that our distance measure is highly correlated with subject ratings in the user study described in Section 4.2.4. Together, these arguments imply that our approach is a valid scheme to quickly retrieve images from a database based on semantic sketches.

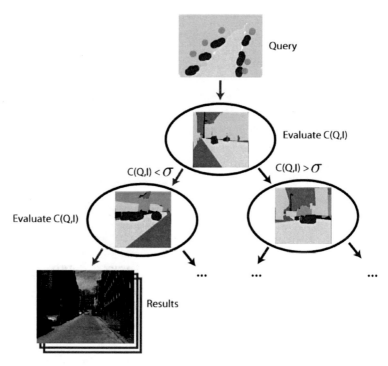

Figure 4.14. Illustration of our decision tree. At each node, the matching cost to a given exemplar is computed. The threshold σ determines whether the left or right child is visited next.

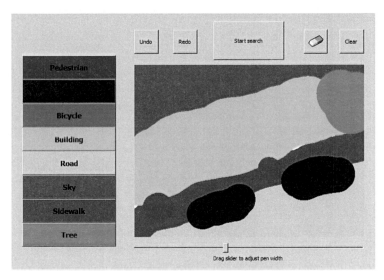

Figure 4.15. Sketch Search user interface. The user chooses objects to include in the scene from the object palette on the left. The canvas depicts a drawn street scene that is used as query for the image search. It shows a street scene containing a road, a sidewalk, two cars, two pedestrians, buildings, trees and sky.

4.2.3 The Sketch Search Interface

We created a painting tool that enables the user to specify the composition of desired images (cf. Figure 4.15). The tool offers a collection of elements that can be included into a query image using semantic brushes. These brushes can represent objects like cars or bicycles, but also image regions like sky or road. To distinguish different brushes, we assign a unique color to each of them. The color value itself is not relevant, since color is used only to denote the type of an object, not its appearance. Which brushes are available depends on the labels found in the current image database. For our evaluations, we used the eight classes in the StreetScenes database.

The sketching interface offers semantic brushes corresponding to the classes in the dataset

111

To create a query image, the user selects scene elements and draws them onto a canvas. The handling of the tool resembles that of common image editing programs. This way of composing a scene is intuitive and self-explanatory, as confirmed by the participants in our user study (see Section 4.2.4).

Users do not have to draw the shape of the objects, thus reducing the required drawing capabilities

To specify an object, it is not necessary to draw its precise shape. It is sufficient to mark the region in the image where instances of its class should occur. Likewise, the actual number of objects drawn is not crucial. By drawing two cars, as shown in the example sketch in Figure 4.15, the user only specifies that the two areas marked as 'car' (red) should contain objects labeled as 'car'. This constraint is fulfilled as long as there is at least one matching object in each of those regions, thus allowing further cars in further image regions.

4.2.4 Evaluation

The StreetScenes database represents a dense sampling of a subregion of the image space. The classes can be roughly labeled automatically, as shown in Section 4.1

In this Section, we present the evaluation of our system. We evaluate and validate our method using the StreetScenes database [14] which contains 3547 images taken in Boston together with annotations of eight major classes: Pedestrian, Bicycle, Car, Street, Sidewalk, Building (including stores), Sky and Trees. Note that our algorithm does not discriminate between objects and semantic regions and deals with them quite naturally. These classes are well suited for our envisioned application since they could potentially be labeled automatically by a computer vision algorithm such as the one proposed in Section 4.1. The number of categories might seem small when compared with the much higher number of classes found for example in the LabelMe database. But, most of the classes from LabelMe are irrelevant for the proposed large-scale image retrieval task, as they have too few occurrences in the database. Obtaining human annotations is expensive and time-consuming, which implies that our algorithm would mainly operate on computer-generated labelings. These annotations would only contain labels for categories that are accessible to vision algorithms, which amounts to a few high-level categories for the near future. Gender specific searches are for example not plausible since algorithmic differentiation between male and female persons is a difficult task. Lastly, it has to be mentioned that there is a strong correlation between classes naturally occurring in images (e.g., 'cars' and 'road' often appear together in an image while 'car' and 'table' do not). This further reduces the number of classes that have to be simultaneously present in a tree.

Algorithmic Evaluation

As first evaluation, we perform automated searches using queries formed from ground truth annotations from the database. We render the results produced by our algorithm and the results obtained when evaluating the cost function for each image individually in Figure 4.16. The results show that our algorithm is able to approximate the linear search through the database with a logarithmic search in our random decision forest.

Our retrieval algorithm can approximate the linear search in logarithmic time

To evaluate the speed of our search, we built trees for a more realistic search setting. By mirroring, shifting and subwindowing random images from the StreetScenes database we created a dataset containing one million images. All timing studies were conducted on a regular office PC with a 3 GHz dual core processor and 2 GB of RAM using our Matlab implementation of the search algorithm. Creating a tree for this dataset takes 3 minutes on average. Queries in this tree take on average 0.23 milliseconds. A linear search through all image descriptors on the other hand takes 17.4 seconds on average making it unsuitable for large-scale application. For more details on computational efficiency, see Figure 4.18.

A query in a set of one million imges takes only 0.23 milliseconds

With eight classes and a 32x32 descriptor, each image can be

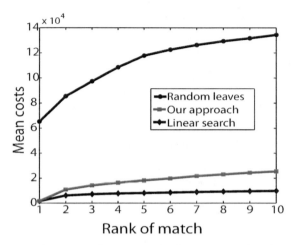

Figure 4.16. Comparison between results for our approach, a linear search through all images and a ranking of random tree leaves according to our cost function. The graph shows the mean costs associated with the top 10 matches.

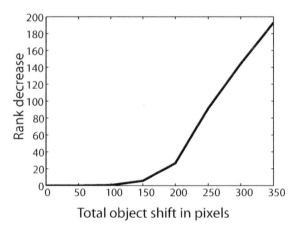

Figure 4.17. The figure shows the decrease in retrieval performance for shifts of object location. The average decrease of matching rank compared to the unshifted queries is plotted on the y-axis.

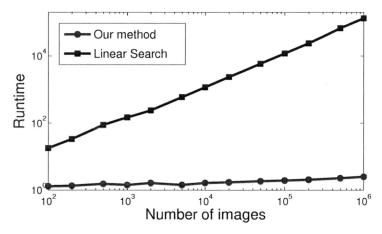

Figure 4.18. Comparison between searches using our method and a linear search in databases of different sizes. Graph axes are logarithmic.

represented using 8096 bytes. This means that a million images would take up 8 GB of memory. This memory problem is present for every image retrieval system, as it needs to keep the image descriptors in memory during runtime. Fortunately, due to the linear nature of the distance transformation, the dimensionality can be greatly reduced using a principle component analysis (PCA). Using PCA we can encode 99% of the variance of the descriptors with just 34 dimensions for this highly redundant dataset. When stored in a single precision float vector, the compressed descriptor takes up only 136 bytes. The evaluation of the cost function is then preceded by a matrix multiplication and addition of the means to project the principle component scores of the descriptors back into the image annotation space. This has to be calculated only $\log n$ times for each tree, thus not critically influencing the runtime. This effectively removes the memory problem, making our algorithm applicable for large scale image search problems.

The descriptors can be compressed to 136 bytes per image using PCA

Robustness against variation in object position can compensate for errors during sketching

Insensitivity to variation in object positions in query images is crucial to provide a level of robustness that is needed to deal with the low fidelity of user sketches (see Section 4.2.5). We evaluated the robustness of our system by shifting the positions of object classes in horizontal or vertical direction by a random amount. However, we set the total number of pixels that all object classes were shifted in one image to a fixed value. In this case, a shift by 320 pixels means that each of the eight object classes we use are shifted by 40 pixels on average. Figure 4.17 shows the decrease in retrieval performance with respect to the original queries. For smaller shifts up to approximately 150 pixels, the results differ only slightly from those obtained by the original queries. Query images had a size of 320x320 pixels, so shifting an object class by a large distance can result in its complete removal from the scene. This effect contributes to the steeper performance decrease at shifts of ca. 200 pixels in total. The evaluation shows that our algorithm is robust against variations in the sketched object location up to a certain degree. Variations beyond 200 pixels can be expected to be intentional.

User Study

A user study examines the validity of the approach in a psychophysical context

In this Section, we show that our approach retrieves images that are not only good in an algorithmic sense but also in a user-subjective sense, which is of key importance for a retrieval system. We performed a user study to evaluate the subjective quality of our algorithm. Ten participants (7 female, 3 male, mean age was 25.6) took part in this study. On average, each participant did 45.7 trials each taking a mean of 53 seconds. To ensure that participants would sketch different images in each trial, they were shown an 'inspiration' image taken randomly from the StreetScenes database for one second before the drawing phase started. The subjects were explicitly instructed to take this image solely as an inspiration and

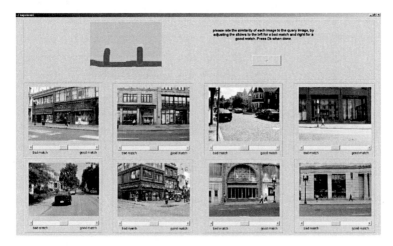

Figure 4.19. Example query and resulting images in the GUI from our user study. The third image in the first row and the first image in the second row are random images, our algorithm's best matches are the second image in the first row and the last in the second row.

not to search for this image explicitly. In the drawing phase, users then sketched an image using the tool described in Section 4.2.3. The resulting sketch served as input for our algorithm, which returned images using a forest consisting of 20 trees.

For the evaluation phase, we selected the four best matches retrieved by our algorithm and the worst and median matches retrieved by our algorithm. Together with two images picked from the database randomly we presented the images simultaneously at randomized positions in the GUI shown in Figure 4.19. Note that 'worst' and 'median' here does not refer to the worst/median match in the whole database but just in the subset (on average 54 images) returned by the search through the forest. Participants were then asked to rate the similarity of the images to their sketch on a scale of 1 (bad match) to 7 (good match). Participants were explicitly instructed not to rate the similarity to the original 'inspirational'

Participants rated the similarity between the retrieved images and their sketches

117

image, which might have created confounds when users remember only certain details about the images.

The top matches received significantly higher ratings

For the analysis of the experimental data, ratings were normalized to a mean of zero and standard deviation of one. We then calculated the average participant rating for each of the seven classes of shown images (best match, second/third/fourth best match, mean match, worst match, random image). The results are visualized in Figure 4.20. A post-hoc Scheffé test ($\alpha = 1\%$) between the means confirms, that participants gave significantly higher ratings to images that our algorithm considered to be good matches than to random images or bad matches. Furthermore, the average rating for the best match is significantly better than the rest, while the second, third, and fourth matches are statistically equal. The mean rating for a 'median' match is significantly worse than the top-matches and significantly better than the worst and random matches. The difference between the random conditions and the worst match approaches significance. This is to be expected as the worst of the retrieved images often did not contain all sketched classes.

$C(Q, I)$ correlates strongly with user ratings

We furthermore analyzed the relation between the algorithm's cost function and the participants' ratings directly. In Figure 4.21, we visualize the mean costs over all query results compared to the average participant ratings for them. The plot y-axis is normalized to one standard deviation of all participants' replies. There is a strong correlation between the two, which is partly due to the cost term κ, which penalizes the absence of objects in bad matches.

The retrieved images and the sketch tool received high subjective ratings

Finally, we asked participants explicitly for their subjective satisfaction with the system. Their ratings for the usability of our sketching tool on a scale of 1 (bad) to 10 (good) resulted in a mean of 7.4. The subjective amount of well-matching results among the shown images (including the two random, 'worst' and 'median' match) was 30.3%. We asked participants explicitly for their sub-

118

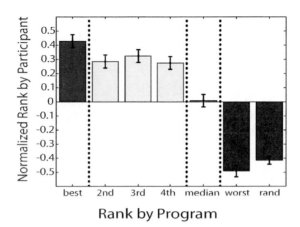

Figure 4.20. Normalized ratings of participants for our algorithm's top four matches, the 'median' and 'worst' match (see text) and two random images. Errorbars denote standard error. Colors indicate a grouping of bars: bar heights in different groups are significantly different while bar heights in the same group are not.

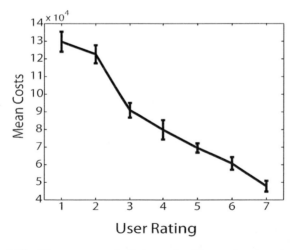

Figure 4.21. The average costs that our algorithm assigns to potential matches show a strong correlation with participant ratings for these matches (1=bad, 7=good match). Errorbars denote standard error.

119

jective satisfaction with the system. Their ratings for usability of our sketching tool on a scale of 1 (bad) to 10 (good) resulted in a mean of 7.3. Together, these results confirm that our algorithmic definition of a good match coincides with the human intuition, allowing our system to yield user-relevant results.

4.2.5 Limitations of Sketch Search

Users produced a lot of suboptimal sketches including birds eye views and impossible scene compositions

Our user study showed that the manual generative abilities of participants are considerably worse than their visual discriminative abilities. Figure 4.22 shows an example of an image and corresponding sketch a user has drawn during the study, which fails to capture the image structure of the inspirational image and represents an impossible semantic composition. Seeing as people are able to copy an image shown during the sketching phase, the problem with bad sketches like these seem to occur when users have to create a 2-D representation of a 3-D scene they have in mind. This poses a general problem to most systems that rely on sketch-based interfaces. Such systems need to find an image, matching the one the user has in mind, based solely on a potentially inaccurate sketch. Our system addresses this problem by requiring only very rough semantic sketches and a distance-transformation-based feature space, which suppresses the errors users make during sketching.

The suboptimal sketching performance limits the applicability of retrieval schemes that require more detailed sketches

When looking at the errors in perspective the users make during drawing, we feel that our very rough sketching interface is already at the upper bound of what can be expected from average users. More complex sketching systems for purposes such as 'Photomontage' allow users to create visually pleasing images with arbitrary scene compositions. However, they only work if the user is able to produce a sensible perspective composition, otherwise they can only create an unrealistic image. Our system cannot create images *de-novo* but is able to find sensible matches very efficiently and ro-

Figure 4.22. Failure case: 'inspirational' image at the top left and sketch created from it in the user study on the bottom left; on the right the four best matches. For some of the bad user sketches (e.g., with impossible perspective as here), no reasonable matches can be found in the database, resulting in bad results. Colors indicate sketched class (brown='building', gray='street' and 'sidewalk', blue='sky'). Images taken from the MIT Street Scenes database [14].

bustly. We feel that automatically creating and annotating large databases of images is a better way to retrieve images matching what the user had in mind. Similar results on participants imprecision in reproducing the perspective of previously seen scene images has also been found in psychophysical studies such as [122].

4.2.6 Conclusion and Outlook

The previous Sections have presented a novel system for content-based image retrieval employing semantic sketches. By utilizing a straight-forward cost function and a decision tree with guaranteed depth of $O(\log n)$, we are able to provide a very fast tool that is able to operate in a webscale context. Our system still yields comparable results to a linear search thus being applicable for large scale image databases. In our user study, we have demonstrated that our system and cost function are efficient and return images matching what the user drew. These factors imply that our system is useful for image retrieval in large, labeled databases.

A future line of research could investigate the extension to more object classes in different scenes while paying attention to the co-occurrences between the two (the class 'road' will rarely occur in an indoor image). Solving these problems and providing efficient semantic retrieval tools will be a major challenge for computer vision as the number of available images grows rapidly. The integration of an automatic scene annotation algorithm could allow the operation on real images from the Internet while providing valuable feedback for the design and optimization of image labeling methods.

4.3 Detectability of Pedestrians

Apart from image retrieval, driver assistance systems are another important and interesting area of applications for computer vision systems. The main goal of driver assistance systems is to make traffic safer for all participants e.g. by providing feedback about possibly dangerous situations or even by actively intervening to avoid collisions. One major source of dangers are collisions between cars and pedestrians. According to the BAST [123], there were 31.647 traffic accidents involving pedestrians in Germany in 2009. Consequently, driver assistance systems usually aim to detect pedestrians and inform the driver about possible risks. Over the course of the last several years, pedestrian detection and tracking was a very active field of research and major advances have been made so far (e.g. [33, 82]). Even though these approaches yield impressive results, they are still not able to match human performance. At first glance, this seems to undermine the possible usefulness of such driver assistance systems, since the computer would use worse input data than the driver, but would have to accomplish a better prediction of possible risks. However, in case of distracted drivers who do not pay the full attention to the road or in conditions with bad visibility artificial vision systems might prove useful. If other modalities, such as infrared cameras or data from a laser-rangefinder, are taken into account, it is reasonable to expect computer vision pedestrian detection algorithms to outperform humans.

Driver assistance systems could provide valuable information in critical situations

Finding the pedestrians that are relevant for the driving task is crucial but only one part of a useful driver assistance system. An open question from the field of human-computer-interfaces (HCI) is how information is best presented to a driver in a minimally intrusive fashion while still presenting all relevant information, thus allowing the driver to avoid collisions with as little distractions as

We aim to estimate the probability that a pedestrian will not be detected by a driver

Figure 4.23. The notion of detectability measures the ease with which pedestrians can be detected in an image. The pedestrian on the right (green) is easily detected, the one in the center (yellow) is harder to detect because of the difficult lighting conditions. The marked pedestrian (red) on the left has a very low detectability. Predicting these detectabilities allows a driver assistance system to better estimate which pedestrians might be in danger.

possible. For example, drawing attention to all pedestrians in the field of view of the driver by e.g. highlighting their outline using a head up display would probably be very distracting and consequently not useful. Thus, the question arises to which pedestrians a driver assistance system should divert the attention of the driver. Risk assessment is a difficult problem, but one that can be done quite well by the driver. The pedestrians that therefore are in most danger are most likely those that have not been noticed by the driver. Consequently, we propose the idea that it would be best to distribute attention to pedestrians that are likely to not have been noticed by the driver. To this end, we introduce a novel computer vision system, which is able to predict the detectability of pedestrians in natural scenes.

4.3.1 State-of-the-Art

To the best of our knowledge, this study is the first in proposing an approach that estimates the detectabilities of pedestrians for HMI-optimization, using a computer vision approach. Most closely related is the recent work by Pomarjanschi et al. [121] who used gaze tracking during a driving task in a virtual reality setting to estimate the pedestrians that were likely to have been missed by the driver. Their study, however, neglected the visual properties of the pedestrian appearance and its scene context, which are likely to influence the detectability of pedestrians. Doshi and Trivedi [37] introduced an approach combining gaze tracking with analysis of the environment, using computer vision to predict driver attention. Similarly, Fletcher et al. [48] have investigated driver gaze tracking in the context of driver assistance systems. Based on a related idea, Spain and Perona [145] measure and predict the "importance" of objects in an image, i.e., the order in which they will be named by a human observer. Pinneli et al. [118] use a Bayesian framework to predict the perceived "interest" of an object using various factors such as location, contrast and color.

Related Work is mostly based on gaze tracking

Most approaches to driver assistance systems address the problem of collision avoidance by detecting (e.g. [33, 85, 106, 116]) and tracking pedestrians (e.g. [2, 142]), recently even using virtual reality scenarios to create ground truth data as in [97]. Furthermore, pedestrian pose estimation, which can yield valuable information about the future path of persons, has received considerable attention from the computer vision community lately [1, 31, 40, 111]. Integrating this high-level information with the results from our approach could drive an internal simulation of the driver assistance system that predicts the future risks of the current situation and the pedestrians in it (c.f. the research regarding risk horizon estimation by e.g. Laugier et al. [50, 79]). Recently, there has

Driver assistance systems so far focus mainly on pedestrian detection, tracking and pose estimation or risk horizon prediction

125

also been interest in human factors of driver assistance problems, which is closely related to our approach. For example, Fletcher et al. [48] have investigated driver gaze tracking in the context of driver assistance systems and Castrillón-Santana and Vuong [23] have proposed a pedestrian detection scheme based on psychophysical data.

4.3.2 Measuring Pedestrian Detectability

'Detectability' is the likelihood that the position of a pedestrian can be correctly reported after 100ms exposure

The first step to create and evaluate an algorithm that estimates pedestrian detectability is to create a dataset containing pedestrians with their associated detectabilities. However, prior to measuring it, we need a concrete working definition of the detectability of a pedestrian. Humans are almost perfect at finding people in images when there are no time constraints (except in the most difficult scenarios such as finding Waldo), but this does not imply that all pedestrians are equally easy to find in an image. In a driving assistance context, it cannot be assumed that the driver will always devote his full attention to searching for pedestrians (which would be bad for all persons in cars or on bicycles). Consequently, the definition of the detectability of a pedestrian we suggest here, is the probability that the position of a pedestrian in an image can be reported correctly by a human observer if the image has been presented for only 100 milliseconds (see Equation 4.8). We opted for the relatively brief presentation time to ensure that only very little high level cognitive processing is taking place and to prevent eye movements (saccades) from having an impact on the perception of the image. Usual saccade latency is about 200ms (see [22, 86]) and even ultra-rapid saccades (e.g. [61, 75]) have a latency of 80ms-100ms and a duration of over 50ms which is considerably longer than the stimulus presentation time. This definition of detectability captures the idea of the ease of detection of a pedestrian in an image 'at a glance'. We imply that this detectability is highly correlated with the probability that a distracted driver (or one that is not paying full attention to the street) will overlook the pedestrian, which are situations in which a driver assistance system should step in and alert the driver to a possibly dangerous situation.

$$\mathcal{D}(\text{Pedestrian}) = p \left(\begin{array}{c} \text{Pedestrian position can be} \\ \text{reported after 100ms} \end{array} \right) \qquad (4.8)$$

We performed a psychophysical experiment to obtain a set of pedestrians with their according detectabilities $\mathcal{D}(\text{Pedestrian})$'s. To guarantee validity, a dataset that contains labeled pedestrians in a natural setting was chosen. The MIT StreetScenes dataset [14] is well suited for the task since it contains labeled pedestrians in a wide variety of poses and contexts and under many different lighting conditions. Furthermore, it includes a large number of images containing two or more pedestrians, which is also important since we assume that a higher number of distracting pedestrians might reduce the overall detectability. The StreetScenes database suffers from several drawbacks, as mentioned earlier in Section 4.1. However, these are not as detrimental in the context of this experiment since we only need a few hundred images from the dataset of over 3500. This enabled us to select the images for the experiment by hand and only pick those images that have high quality annotations.

Detectability of pedestrians is measured in an experiment

For the experiment we selected a total of 626 images from the StreetScenes database. 142 contained no pedestrians, 245 contained exactly one pedestrian and 239 contained two or more pedestrians. One trial of the experiment consisted of the following stages: First the participants were shown a fixation cross for 500ms. Then the image from the database was presented for 100ms, followed by a random noise mask for 500ms to prevented any further low-level processing from taking place. After that,

A resulting dataset of 626 pedestrians with associated detectabilities

127

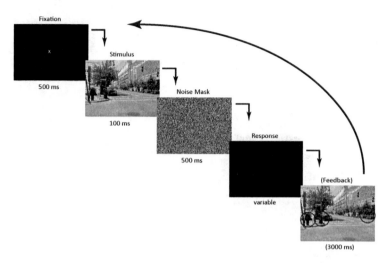

Figure 4.24. The design of the experiment to determine the detectabilities of pedestrians. A fixation cross was presented for 500ms, followed by the test image from the StreetScenes database for 100ms and a noise mask for 500ms to suppress all further low-level processing. During the response phase, participants clicked on all pedestrians they had seen in the image. In one fifth of the trials, feedback about the true positions of all labeled pedestrians in the image was provided for 3 seconds.

a black screen was presented and the participants had to indicate where in the image they perceived pedestrians, by clicking on the locations on the screen with a mouse. A red dot appeared where they clicked. In 20% of the trials chosen randomly, feedback was provided by showing the image once again combined with the ground truth positions of the pedestrians and the responses of the participants. The feedback was given to allow the participants to correct for biases in their responses (without feedback users showed a tendency to click closer to the center of the image). A schematic representation of the experiment is shown in Figure 4.24. The experiment was programmed in Matlab using the Psychophysics Toolbox 3 [19, 77] to ensure accurate timing.

128

Since the rapid presentation times can make this a rather exhausting task for some participants and we wanted to avoid fatigue effects, the users were forced to take a short break every 100 trials. The head position of the participants was fixated 65 centimeters away from the monitor using a chinrest resulting in a horizontal viewing angle of approximately 60°. There was an introduction and a training phase before the experiment to familiarize the participants with the setup and to reduce possible response biases. After the experiment, all participants answered a questionnaire. A total of 11 subjects participated in the experiment, 4 female and 7 male with an average age of 26.4. 10 were right-handed and 1 was left-handed. They took on average 1.5 seconds for the responses.

11 participants took on average 1.5 seconds

Our response method asks the participants to click on the positions where they have seen a pedestrian from memory. This task is prone to several kinds of noise such as: manual imprecision during clicking, inaccurate memory encoding and retrieval and others. To compensate for this, we counted every click in a radius of 100 pixels center of gravity of a pedestrian as a correct detection. For large pedestrians in the foreground, we also accepted clicks on the annotation polygon as a hit (see Figure 4.25). By averaging over all participants' responses, we obtained the detectability characteristics denoted by $\mathcal{D}$(Pedestrian) for each pedestrian.

Clicks in a 100 pixel radius around the pedestrian center counted as correct detections

The average detectability across all pedestrian in our database is 62.97%. A more detailed distribution of detectabilities is shown in the histogram in Figure 4.26. All possible detection probabilities are approximately evenly represented in our database (except for a high number (172) of samples that were correctly detected by all participants). An analysis of the correlations between the percentage of correctly marked pedestrians with the answers given in the questionnaire is summarized in Table 4.6. However, because of the low number of subjects only the correlation with driving experience

Significant correlation of subject performance with driving experience

129

Figure 4.25. Examples of correct (yellow dots) and incorrect (red dots) participant responses in the detectability experiment. The red circle shows the 100 pixel radius around the center of the pedestrian that represents the 'hit zone'. All clicks in that circle were treated as correct detections of that pedestrian. For large pedestrians (center), the whole body also counted as 'hit zone'. In case of multiple pedestrians that are close together (right), ambiguous clicks can occur. Since we are not able to determine post-hoc, which pedestrian was really detected by the user we treat both pedestrians as being 'detected'.

is significant with $p < 0.05$. The correlation with the total number of clicks in all images approaches significance ($p = 0.056$). It is furthermore interesting to notice that neither gender, experience with videogames or the estimated percentage of correct answers as reported by the participants showed any correlation with the true performance (correlations of 0.15, 0.16 and 0.10, respectively).

4.3.3 Predicting Pedestrian Detectability

SVR used to predict the detectability of pedestrians

Our dataset contains a total of 852 samples of pedestrians with associated detectabilities. We split the set into 600 samples for training and the remaining 252 samples were set aside for testing and estimating the validation performance. In order to provide useful information in a driver assistance scenario, we have to prove that a mapping can be learned which is able to reliably and robustly predict the detectabilitiy of pedestrians. The mapping can be realized in terms of a regression function. This is a difficult task since the training data obtained earlier is noisy. Even though the subset of images from the StreetScenes was selected by hand, the

130

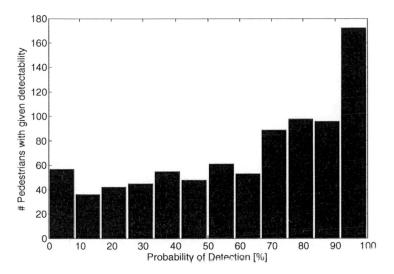

Figure 4.26. Histogram of the count of pedestrians for the different detection probabilities. There is a high number of pedestrians (172) that were correctly reported by all participants.

Age	−0.28
Response Time	0.39
Proficiency with Computer	−0.24
Regularity of Driving	0.64
Estimated % correct	0.10
Estimated % of images with more than one pedestrian	0.42
Total # of clicks	0.59
Proficiency with video games	0.16
Gender	0.15

Table 4.6. Correlations between the responses from questionnaires and the number of correctly detected pedestrians.

images and annotations are not perfect, the manual imprecision of the participants can lead to false detections or misses and in situations where a group of pedestrians is close together the clicks of the users can be ambiguous (see Figure 4.25). To counteract the noise in the data, we needed to train a robust regression that operates on a set of robust features. We chose Support Vector Regression (SVR, c.f. [38, 137]) with an RBF kernel as a regressor as it has proven to produce state-of-the-art results even on small and noisy datasets. We employed the freely available libsvm [24] implementation to train and test our SVRs. We extracted a large battery of possibly useful features from the dataset (Table 4.7 shows a list of all features).

Name	# Dim	Description
$pHoG$	168	Pyramidial Histogram of Oriented Gradients Descriptor as described in [17]
Pos	2	Absolute position of the pedestrian in image coordinates
$Area$	1	Area of the bounding box of the annotation of the pedestrians
$PedCount$	1	Total number of pedestrians in the image
$PedMean$	1	Average brightness of the pedestrian
$PedStd$	1	Standard Deviation of the pixels in the bounding box associated with the pedestrian after transforming it to grayscale
$DiffMean$	1	Difference in mean color between the bounding box of the pedestrian and its context (we define the context as a box three times the width and double the height of the pedestrian around the center of the pedestrian (see Figure 4.27))
$DiffStd$	1	Difference in standard deviation between the bounding box of the pedestrian and its context
$DiffHist$	51	Earth Mover Distance (EMD e.g. [132]) between the grayscale color histograms drawn from the pedestrian and its context

DiffRGBHist	51	The EMD between the RGB color histograms drawn from the pedestrian and its context
DiffLABHist	81	The EMD between the LAB (c.f. [69]) color histograms drawn from the pedestrian and its context
Dist2Center	1	Distance from the center of the pedestrian to the center of the image
Dist2Ped	1	Distance from the center of the pedestrian to the center of the closest other pedestrian in the image
Dist2Car	1	Distance from the center of the pedestrian to the center of the center of the nearest annotated car in the image
PixelPerClass	8	Number of pixels in the image that belong to each of the eight annotated classes
PixelPerFG	3	Number of pixels in the image that each of the three foreground classes (pedestrian, car, bicycle)
FixColor	1	Mean brightness of a 15×15 area around the fixation point in the image
DiffFix	1	Difference in brightness between the fixation point and the mean color of the pedestrian
mfThres	1	After resizing the image in the bounding box around the pedestrian to 100×50, we computed the flux flow $\mathcal{F}$ as described in Section 2.2. mfThres is the number of pixels whose flux flow is above a threshold of 1 and represents the level of symmetry in this area
mfCount	1	Number of SCIPs found in the resized image patch containing the pedestrian
mfMaxScale	1	Largest scale of a SCIP in the resized image patch (see Section 2.3.2)
mfMeanScale	1	Average scale of a SCIP in the resized image patch (see Section 2.3.2)

Table 4.7. Features used for the regression of the detectabilities. First column denotes the name of the feature, the second one its dimensionality and the third one provides a short description.

Symmetry features are important cues since pedestrians are highly symmetrical entities

Features encoding the symmetry of the pedestrians such as *mfThres*, *mfCount*, *mfMaxScale* and *mfMeanScale* are of special interest to us. As observed by e.g. [11, 20], shape-centered features that encode the symmetry can be very powerful for pedestrian detection and tracking since pedestrians are highly symmetric shapes. Therefore, we expect pedestrians that violate this assumption and do not possess a symmetric shape to be harder to detect by humans. Furthermore, several features depend on the difference between the pedestrian and its context (for a critical discussion of context for object detection see Wolf et al. [161]). We define the context of a pedestrian as a box three times the width and double the height of the pedestrian, located around the center of the pedestrian (see Figure 4.27).

The high dimensionality makes a feature selection necessary to avoid the *curse of dimensionality*

The total dimensionality of all combined features is 378. We normalized the feature vectors to ensure that each dimension has a mean of zero and a standard deviation of one to prevent a single dimension dominating the distance measure (variance normalization). Similar to Section 4.1, the number of dimensions is very high when compared to the number of training examples resulting in the *curse of dimensionality* (see [8, 9, 12]). Analog to Section 4.1, we addressed this problem by using our probabilistic brute-force feature selection scheme to train the SVR parameters (the Slack Variable ϵ, the regularization parameter C and the σ of the RBF Kernel) and select the optimal subset of features simultaneously. Table 4.8 shows, which features were finally selected by our feature selection scheme. The dimensionality of the final descriptor is 68 and contains two of our shape-centered features indicating the importance of symmetry for human pedestrian detection.

After performing the feature selection and the parameter optimization, we learned a model on the training data and predicted the detectabilities of all pedestrians in the test dataset:

Figure 4.27. The context of a pedestrian (gray) is the box twice the height of the pedestrian and three times its width around the center of the pedestrian. Image adapted from the MIT Street Scenes database [14].

Name	Dimensionality
Area	1
PedCount	1
DiffStd	1
DiffHist	51
Dist2Center	1
Dist2Ped	1
DiffFix	1
PedMean	1
PixelPerClass	8
mfCount	1
mfMeanScale	1

Table 4.8. The result of our feature selection scheme. The reduced feature vector contains only 68 dimensions.

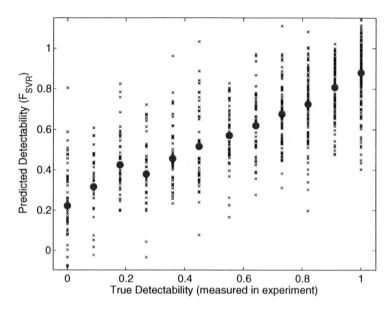

Figure 4.28. Prediction performance of the trained regressor. The plot shows the predicted detectability versus the true detectability (as assessed by our experiment) for all images in the test dataset. Blue circles show the means for each level of ground-truth detectability. The means show a clear linear correlation.

$$F_{\mathrm{SVR}}(\mathbf{X}) = \mathcal{D}, \qquad\qquad (4.9)$$

F_{SVR} predicts the detectability of a pedestrian based on the descriptor $\mathbf{X}$

where F_{SVR} is the SVR we trained to predict the detectability $\mathcal{D}$ for a pedestrian with the feature vector $\mathbf{X}$. The results are plotted in Figure 4.28. The mean squared error of the prediction is 0.04 and the R^2 value for the correlation is 0.62. Due to the above mentioned noise in the data, this might already be very close to the maximal performance.

136

4.3.4 Optimizing the Focus of Attention

In order to demonstrate that being able to predict the detectability of a pedestrian could be useful we have to show its applicability in a real world scenario. We did this by optimizing the position of the fixation cross during the experiment. This is a proxy-task for directing the attention of the driver by an assistance system to a certain position in such a way that all pedestrians in the scene are optimally detected. Without knowing the detectabilities, a driver assistance system would have to assume that all pedestrians in the image are equally difficult to spot and would consequently shift the attention of the driver to the center of gravity between all pedestrians. Our system on the other hand can predict the optimal position of the fixation cross according to the learned regressor. We evaluated the regressor densely at all image locations and predicted the detectabilities of all pedestrians (the four features Position, Dist2Center, FixColor and DiffFix depend on the position of the fixation cross resulting in different predictions for different image locations). Figure 4.29 shows examples of the mean detectability of all pedestrians in the image, depending on the position of the fixation cross.

Prediction of the optimal fixation cross position demonstrates the usefulness of the estimation of detectabilities

We then determine the optimal fixation point as the position where the mean detectability of all pedestrians in the current image is maximized. This scheme yields different fixation points than the fixation point prediction based on the center between the pedestrians (see Figure 4.30).

Based on these two kinds of fixation cross locations (predicted and mean), we set up another experiment to evaluate whether our method actually yields an increased overall detectability. We selected 115 images from the database for which the two kinds of fixation points differed by at least 50 pixels. We repeated the experiment described in the previous Section, but this time with

Evaluating the performance with and without knowing the detectability of pedestrians

137

Figure 4.29. Shown are pairs of images and corresponding heat maps of the predicted detectability for all possible fixation cross positions. Colors indicate the mean of the predicted detectability for all pedestrians in the image. The top row shows that our approach picks up on the large pedestrian in the foreground that is easily perceived and shifts the focus of attention to the harder to find pedestrians in the background.

Figure 4.30. Examples of the two different methods of predicting the position of the fixation cross. The red dot indicates the center between all labeled pedestrians in the image while the blue dot is the optimal fixation point according to our regressor. In the two cases here, the regressor has estimated that one person will be particularly hard to detect and that the focus should be shifted more closer to that pedestrian.

variable positioning of the fixation crosses.

To compare the two kinds of fixation locations better, we used the mirrored versions of the images as well, and presented the two different fixation cross positions on the two versions of the same image. The pairing of fixation cross type, whether the image was mirrored or not and the presentation order was randomized for each participant. We furthermore added trials in which the fixation cross position was unrelated to the image content as a baseline condition. To ensure that the distribution of fixation cross positions in the baseline condition is comparable to the other two conditions, we used the predicted fixation cross locations from one of the other conditions but from a different image to determine the location of the fixation cross.

Mirrored images included to allow direct comparison

Each of the ten participants (five female and five male, with a mean age of 24.6) did 550 trials and completed a questionnaire afterwards. The head position of the participants was again fixated 65 centimeters away from the monitor using a chinrest resulting in a horizontal viewing angle of approximately 60°. Three of the subjects reported afterwards that they had noticed that some of the images were presented twice in mirrored conditions. Figure 4.31 shows the percentage of correctly reported pedestrians across all trials as a function of hit radius (the radius of the ring in Figure 4.25 for all three kinds of fixation point locations (predicted, centered and random)). The Figure shows that our regressor clearly outperforms the fixation cross positioning at the center between all pedestrians and the random baseline condition.

The predicted fixation cross position yields the best performance

4.3.5 Conclusions and Outlook

In this Section, we presented and evaluated the novel idea of estimating the detectability of pedestrians in natural images using computer vision techniques. We trained a regressor to predict these detectabilities and were able to show that estimating the

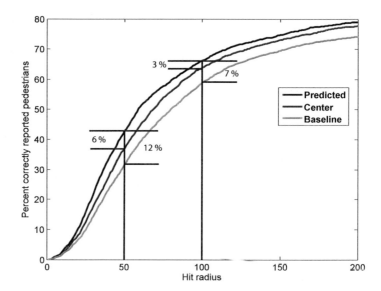

Figure 4.31. Portion of pedestrians whose position was correctly reported and counted as a 'hit' as a function of the radius of the disc associated with the pedestrian. Our method based on the results of the regressor (red line) outperforms the methods that have no access to the detectability of the pedestrians (center of all pedestrians in the image (blue line) and random fixation cross position (green line)). The 6% absolute performance increase equals a relative improvement of performance by 16% over the 'center' method.

140

detectabilities can yield considerable improvements in the overall detection rates of pedestrians.

Future investigations could aim to evaluate the detectabilities of pedestrians in a dynamic context. This would require either videos with high quality annotations or a virtual reality setup. A virtual reality setup would also allow closer control over the parameters that influence the detectability of pedestrians, the controlled introduction of distractors and state-dependent estimations (e.g. with respect to the current body pose of the pedestrian). Furthermore, estimating critical situations in user studies could provide valuable feedback for pedestrian detection and scene annotation schemes e.g. by indicating in which conditions correct detections are especially important.

5

Discussion

We can only see a short distance ahead, but we can see plenty there that needs to be done.

Alan Turing

5.1 Summary

This thesis presented an investigation of shape-centered representations from low-level interest points to high-level applications. Chapter 2 introduced a novel set of shape-centered interest points (SCIPs), which are interest points formed at locations of high local image symmetry. Local symmetry is obtained by computing the flux flow $\mathcal{F}$ on the normalized gradient vector flow (GVF) field V_N. We sample SCIPs from the local extrema of this flux flow field. The interest points possess scale and rotation invariance by virtue of a local scale and orientation estimation. We demonstrated their robustness against noise and clutter, which makes them applicable for higher-level computer vision algorithms. Evaluation proved that the SCIP carry complementary information to traditional corner-based interest points. We have furthermore shown that they measure up to other state-of-the-art interest point detectors with respect to the information that they encode.

Based on the SCIP feature framework, Chapter 3 introduces two schemes that combine low-level information to obtain a robust mid-level representation of the image content. First, Section 3.1 introduces a novel way to group corner-based interest points at the SCIPs. This grouping yields very powerful descriptors by integrating information from the corners. The grouping scheme allows us to combine the advantages of SCIPs (tight connection to a single shape, robustness against noise and clutter) with the advantages of corner interest points such as SIFT (a strong descriptor of the local edge-structure) and the resulting meta-features offer a powerful state-of-the-art mid-level representation. Section 3.2 presents a novel set of superpixels based on the medial features described before. These superpixels yield an oversegmentation of the image into visually coherent regions. Evaluations show that our superpixels outperfom state-of-the-art oversegmentations with respect to their similarity to human segmentations, thus yielding a valid starting point for the subsequent applications that act as an interface between humans and machines.

Using these robust mid-level representation avails the opportunity to create useful applications that link algorithmic vision to human perception thus allowing us to evaluate and optimize the computer vision methods based on actual humans in-the-loop. To this end, Chapter 4 presents three high level applications that are based on the shape-centered representations developed in the earlier chapters. First, Section 4.1 lays the ground-work by introducing a multi-class scene annotation pipeline. This pipeline produces dense semantic labels of images. The first step is a local classification step based on support vector machines. Then,

144

conditional random fields are used in a global optimization step that smoothes the hypotheses generated by the local prediction step and produces a globally valid annotation taking into account contextual constraints from the spatial neighborhood. The results of such a labeling pipeline can then be used in a human-machine-interaction context where humans can benefit from computer vision, thus bridging the gap from low-level features to applications. Section 4.2 presents such an application that retrieves images based on semantic sketches. Image retrieval is an important problem in the digital age where millions of new images become available every day. Our novel approach makes use of image semantics (like the ones generated by our scene labeling pipeline) to find images that are semantically similar to a query. An experiment demonstrated the validity of our approach and exhaustive evaluation demonstrates that our retrieval scheme can work in a webscale scenario with millions of images. Finally, Section 4.3 details a novel approach for estimating the detectability of pedestrians in a driver assistance context and investigates the factors influencing the detectability of pedestrians of both humans and machines. Here, the high-level image semantics estimated by systems such as our scene labeling pipeline are necessary to estimate parameters (in this case the detectability of a pedestrian) that are valuable for the humans being assisted by an automatic driver assistance device. We performed an experiment, which evaluates the detectability of pedestrians and trained a regressor to predict the detectability for yet unseen pedestrians. Subsequently, we performed a second experiment in which we could demonstrate that our calibrated framework can provide useful information for a driver assistance system by e.g. directing the attention to a position in the scene where the overall detection rates of all pedestrians will be maximized.

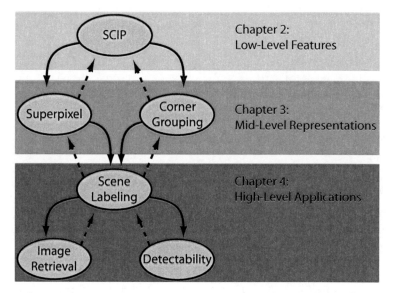

Figure 5.1. Possibilities of feedback throughout the different layers of the framework. Dotted lines indicated where knowledge gained from the interaction with humans can be fed back to lower level components.

5.2 Outlook

In this thesis, we achieved the connection from low-level computer vision to human-machine-interaction in a mostly feed-forward manner. Future lines of investigation will look at the human factors on the highest levels and produce feedback through the three layers of our framework. By exploiting the link between human perception and computer vision, established in the application layer, we can modify and optimize the performances of the lower layers. Figure 5.1 shows the workflow from the beginning with additional links indicating where valuable feedback could be used to improve components of earlier layers.

For example, evaluating the perceptual relevance for the different classes in the context of the detectability or the sketch search experiment will yield different relevances for the different classes. This means that the loss function of the classifiers in the scene labeling stage should be adapted to reflect, which classes have to be recognized with high precision and for which classes a rough detection is sufficient (e.g. the position of the sky might not be as important as the position of the road in a driver assistance context). Further feedback can be generated from the annotation stage to the mid-level representation stage. Here, knowledge about the object class and position can be used to e.g. fuse superpixels or update the grouping of SIFTs. With semantic knowledge at the level of superpixels of grouped corner interest points feedback to the low-level feature layer would be possible including for example suppression of clutter edges in the descriptors or local contrast normalization for static image analysis but also in a tracking context. Generally, these feedback paths introduce the human-factor into computer vision and are a very promising direction in current computer vision research. They will produce very valuable insights into algorithmic vision as well as human perception in the coming years.

A different future line of research could investigate the extension of such a framework to dynamic scenes. The SCIP and the mid-level representations could be extended to image sequences. Linking the features and grouped corner points from one frame to the next, would allow robust tracking algorithms to follow objects in videos. Furthermore, investigating the detectability estimation from Section 4.3 in a dynamic context is an important line of future inquiry to make the system applicable to real driver assistance scenarios.

List of Figures

LIST OF FIGURES

Bibliography

[1] A. Agarwal and B. Triggs. Monocular human motion capture with a mixture of regressors. In *Computer Vision and Pattern Recognition - Workshops*, pages 72–80, 2005.

[2] M. Andriluka, S. Roth, and B. Schiele. People-tracking-by-detection and people-detection-by-tracking. In *Computer Vision and Pattern Recognition*, pages 1–8, 2008.

[3] C. Arcelli and G. S. di Baja. Ridge points in euclidean distance maps. *Pattern Recognition Letters*, 13(4):237 – 243, 1992.

[4] Aristotle. *Categories*. selfpublished, 322 BC.

[5] D. H. Ballard. Generalizing the hough transform to detect arbitrary shapes. *Readings in computer vision: issues, problems, principles, and paradigms*, 13:714–725, 1987.

[6] K. Barnard and M. Johnson. Word sense disambiguation with pictures. *Artificial Intelligence*, 167:13–30, 2005.

[7] H. Bay, A. Ess, T. Tuytelaars, and L. Van Gool. Speeded-up robust features. *Computer Vision and Image Understanding*, 110(3):346–359, 2008.

[8] R. Bellman. *Dynamic Programming*. Dover Publications, March 1957.

[9] R. E. Bellman. *Adaptive control processes - A guided tour*. Princeton University Press, 1961.

[10] S. Berretti, A. D. Bimbo, and P. Pala. Retrieval by shape similarity with perceptual distance and effective indexing. *IEEE Transaction on Multimedia*, 2(4):225–239, 2000.

[11] M. Bertozzi, A. Broggi, R. Chapuis, F. Chausse, A. Fascioli, and A. Tibaldi. Shape-based pedestrian detection and localization. In *International Conference on Intelligent Transportation Systems*, pages 328–333, 2003.

[12] K. Beyer, J. Goldstein, R. Ramakrishnan, and U. Shaft. When is "nearest neighbor" meaningful? In *International Conference on Database Theory*, pages 217–235, 1999.

[13] S. Bileschi and L. Wolf. Image representations beyond histograms of gradients: The role of gestalt descriptors. In *Computer Vision and Pattern Recognition*, pages 1–8, 2007.

[14] S. M. Bileschi. *Streetscenes: towards scene understanding in still images*. PhD thesis, Massachusetts Institute of Technology, Cambridge, MA, USA, 2006.

[15] I. Borg and P. Groenen. *Modern Multidimensional Scaling: Theory and Applications*. Springer, 2005.

[16] G. Borgefors. Distance transformations in digital images. In *Computer Vision, Graphics, and Image Processing*, volume 34, pages 344–371, 1986.

[17] A. Bosch, A. Zisserman, and X. Munoz. Representing shape with a spatial pyramid kernel. In *Conference on Image and Video Retrieval*, pages 401–408, 2007.

[18] Y. Boykov, O. Veksler, and R. Zabih. Efficient approximate energy minimization via graph cuts. *Pattern Analysis and Machine Intelligence*, 20(12):1222–1239, 2001.

[19] D. H. Brainard. The psychophysics toolbox. *Spatial Vision*, 10:433–436, 1997.

[20] T. Bücher, C. Curio, H. Edelbrunner, C. Igel, D. Kastrup, I. Leefken, G. Lorenz, A. Steinhage, and W. von Seelen. Image processing and behaviour planning for intelligent vehicles. *Transactions on Industrial Electronics*, 50(1):62–75, 2003.

[21] F. J. Canny. A computational approach to edge detection. *Pattern Analysis and Machine Intelligence*, 8(6):679–698, 1986.

[22] R. H. S. Carpenter. *Movements of the eyes*. Pion, London, 1977.

[23] M. Castrilln-Santana and Q. Vuong. Combining human perception and geometric restrictions for automatic pedestrian detection. In *Current Topics in Artificial Intelligence*, volume 4177, pages 163–170, 2006.

[24] C.-C. Chang and C.-J. Lin. *LIBSVM: a library for support vector machines*, 2001.

[25] O. Chapelle, V. Vapnik, O. Bousquet, and S. Mukherjee. Choosing multiple parameters for support vector machines. *Machine Learning*, 46(1–3):131–159, 2002.

[26] T. Chen, M.-M. Cheng, P. Tan, A. Shamir, and S.-M. Hu. Sketch2photo: Internet image montage. In *SIGGraph Asia*, 2009.

[27] Y. Cheng. Mean shift, mode seeking and clustering. *Pattern Analysis and Machine Intelligence*, 17(8):790–799, 1995.

[28] D. Comaniciu and P. Meer. Mean shift analysis and applications. In *International Conference on Computer Vision*, page 1197, 1999.

[29] M. C. Cooper. The tractability of segmentation and scene analysis. *International Journal of Computer Vision*, 30(1):27–42, 1998.

[30] G. Csurka, C. R. Dance, L. Fan, J. Willamowski, and C. Bray. Visual categorization with bags of keypoints. In *European Conference on Computer Vision - Workshops*, pages 1–22, 2004.

[31] C. Curio. *A learning-based computer vision approach for the inference of articulated motion*. PhD thesis, Ruhr University Bochum, 2004.

[32] C. Curio and D. Engel. A computational mid-level vision approach for shape-specific saliency detection. In *Proceedings of Annual Meeting of the Vision Sciences Society*, volume 10, page 308, 2010.

[33] N. Dalal and B. Triggs. Histograms of oriented gradients for human detection. In *Computer Vision and Pattern Recognition*, volume 2, pages 886–893, 2005.

[34] R. Datta, J. Li, and J. Z. Wang. Content-based image retrieval: approaches and trends of the new age. In *Interna-*

tional Workshop on Multimedia Information Retrieval, pages 253–262, 2005.

[35] H. Deng, W. Zhang, E. Mortensen, T. Dietterich, and L. Shapiro. Principal curvature-based region detector for object recognition. In *Computer Vision and Pattern Recognition*, pages 1–8, 2007.

[36] P. Dimitrov, J. N. Damon, and K. Siddiqi. Flux invariants for shape. *In Computer Vision and Pattern Recognition*, 1:835–841, 2003.

[37] A. Doshi and M. Trivedi. Attention estimation by simultaneous observation of viewer and view. In *Computer Vision and Pattern Recognition Workshops*, pages 21 – 27, 2010.

[38] H. Drucker, C. J. C. Burges, L. Kaufman, A. Smola, and V. Vapnik. Support vector regression machines. In *Advances in Neural Information Processing Systems*, pages 155–161, 1997.

[39] R. O. Duda and P. E. Hart. Use of the hough transformation to detect lines and curves in pictures. *ACM Communications*, 15(1):11–15, 1972.

[40] D. Engel. Learning-based human pose tracking in clutter. Master's thesis, Universität Tübingen, 2006.

[41] D. Engel and C. Curio. Scale-invariant medial features based on gradient vector flow fields. In *International Conference on Pattern Recognition*, 2008.

[42] D. Engel and C. Curio. Shape centered interest points for feature grouping. In *Computer Vision and Pattern Recognition - Workshops*, 2010.

[43] D. Engel, L. Spinello, R. Triebel, R. Siegwart, H. Bülthoff, and C. Curio. Medial features for superpixel segmentation. In *Machine Vision Applications*, pages 248–252, 2009.

[44] J. Fauqueur and N. Boujemaa. Logical query composition from local visual feature thesaurus. In *Workshop on Content-Based Multimedia Indexing*, 2003.

[45] L. Fei-Fei, R. Fergus, and P. Perona. Learning generative visual models from few training examples: An incremental bayesian approach tested on 101 object categories. *Computer Vision and Pattern Recognition*, 12:178, 2004.

[46] L. Fei-Fei, R. Fergus, and P. Perona. One-shot learning of object categories. *Pattern Analysis and Machine Intelligence*, 28(4):594, 2006.

[47] P. F. Felzenszwalb and D. P. Huttenlocher. Efficient graph-based image segmentation. *International Journal of Computer Vision*, 59(2):167–181, 2004.

[48] L. Fletcher, G. Loy, N. Barnes, and A. Zelinsky. Correlating driver gaze with the road scene for driver assistance systems. *Robotics and Autonomous Systems*, 52(1):71 – 84, 2005.

[49] M. Flickner, H. Sawhney, W. Niblack, J. Ashley, Q. Huang, B. Dom, M. Gorkani, J. Hafner, D. Lee, D. Petkovic, D. Steele, and P. Yanker. Query by image and video content: The qbic system. *Computer*, 28(9):23–32, 1995.

[50] C. Fulgenzi, A. Spalanzani, and C. Laugier. Probabilistic motion planning among moving obstacles following typical motion patterns. In *Intelligent Robots and Systems*, pages 4027–4033, 2009.

[51] B. Fulkerson, A. Vedaldi, and S. Soatto. Class segmentation and object localization with superpixel neighborhoods. In *International Conference on Computer Vision*, 2009.

[52] D. Gavrila, U. Franke, C. Wohler, and S. Gorzig. Real time vision for intelligent vehicles. *IEEE Instrumentation Measurement Magazine*, 4(2):22 –27, 2001.

[53] J. J. Gibson. The theory of affordances. In *Perceiving, Acting and Knowing*, 1977.

[54] J. J. Gibson. *The Ecological Approach to Visual Perception*. Lawrence Erlbaum Associates, 1 edition, 1979.

[55] W.-B. Goh and K.-Y. Chan. Shape description using gradient vector field histograms. In *Scale Space Methods in Computer Vision*, pages 1611–3349, 2003.

[56] W.-B. Goh and K.-Y. Chan. The multiresolution gradient vector field skeleton. *Pattern Recognition*, 40:1255–1269, 2007.

[57] K. Grauman and T. Darrell. The pyramid match kernel: Discriminative classification with sets of image features. In *International Conference on Computer Vision*, pages 1458–1465, 2005.

[58] D. M. Greig, B. T. Porteous, and A. H. Seheult. Exact maximum a posteriori estimation for binary images. *Journal of the Royal Statistical Society*, 1:271–279, 1989.

[59] J. M. Hammersley and P. Clifford. Markov random fields in statistics. Course-Notes, 1971.

[60] C. Harris and M. Stephens. A combined corner and edge detector. In *Proceedings of the Fourth Alvey Vision Conference*, pages 147–152, 1988.

[61] J. Haushofer, P. H. Schiller, G. Kendall, W. M. Slocum, and A. S. Tolias. Express saccades: the conditions under which they are realized and the brain structures involved. *Journal of Vision*, 2(7):174–174, 2002.

[62] X. He, R. S. Zemel, and M. . Carreira-perpin. Multiscale conditional random fields for image labeling. In *Computer Vision and Pattern Recognition*, pages 695–702, 2004.

[63] K. Hirata and T. Kato. Query by visual example - content based image retrieval. In *International Conference on Extending Database Technology*, pages 56–71, 1992.

[64] T. K. Ho. Random decision forests. In *International Conference on Document Analysis and Recognition*, page 278, 1995.

[65] D. Hoiem, A. A. Efros, and M. Hebert. Geometric context from a single image. In *International Conference of Computer Vision*, volume 1, pages 654 – 661, 2005.

[66] D. Hoiem, A. A. Efros, and M. Hebert. Closing the loop on scene interpretation. In *Computer Vision and Pattern Recognition*, 2008.

[67] D. Hoiem, A. Stein, A. Efros, and M. Hebert. Recovering occlusion boundaries from a single image. In *International Conference on Computer Vision*, pages 1–8, 2007.

[68] L. Huan and H. Motoda. *Feature Selection for Knowledge Discovery and Data Mining*. Springer, 1998.

[69] R. S. Hunter. Photoelectric color difference meter. *Journal of the Optical Society of America*, 48(12):985–993, 1958.

[70] C. E. Jacobs, A. Finkelstein, and D. H. Salesin. Fast multiresolution image querying. In *International Conference on Computer Graphics and Interactive Techniques*, pages 277–286, 1995.

[71] M. Johnson, G. Brostow, J. Shotton, O. Arandjelovic, V. Kwatra, and R. Cipolla. Semantic photo synthesis. *Computer Graphics Forum*, 25(3):407–413, 2006.

[72] I. T. Jolliffe. *Principal Component Analysis*. Springer, 1986.

[73] W. Kienzle, F. A. Wichmann, B. Scholkopf, and M. O. Franz. Learning an interest operator from human eye movements. In *Computer Vision and Pattern Recognition - Workshop*, page 24, 2006.

[74] B. Kimia and A. Tamrakar. The role of propagation and medial geometry in human vision. *Journal of Physiology*, 97:155–190, 2003.

[75] H. Kirchner and S. J. Thorpe. Ultra-rapid object detection with saccadic eye movements: Visual processing speed revisited. *Vision Research*, 46(11):1762 – 1776, 2006.

[76] S. Kirkpatrick, J. Gelatt, C. D., and M. P. Vecchi. Optimization by simulated annealing. *Science*, 220(4598):671–680, 1983.

[77] M. Kleiner, D. Brainard, and D. Pelli. Whats new in psychtoolbox-3? In *European Conference on Visual Perception*, 2007.

[78] J. D. Lafferty, A. McCallum, and F. C. N. Pereira. Conditional random fields: Probabilistic models for segmenting and labeling sequence data. In *International Conference on Machine Learning*, pages 282–289, 2001.

64644446444444

424242424

242424242424

[79] C. Laugier, S. Petti, D. A. Vasquez Govea, M. Yguel, T. Fraichard, and O. Aycard. Steps towards safe navigation in open and dynamic environments. In *International Conference on Robotics and Automation - Workshop*, 2005.

[80] T. Lee, D. Mumford, R. Romero, and V. Lamme. The role of the primary visual cortex in higher level vision. *Vision Research*, 38:2429–2454, 1998.

[81] B. Leibe, A. Leonardis, and B. Schiele. Combined object categorization and segmentation with an implicit shape model. In *European Conference on Computer Vision - Workshop*, volume 1, pages 17–32, 2004.

[82] B. Leibe, A. Leonardis, and B. Schiele. Robust object detection with interleaved categorization and segmentation. *International Journal of Computer Vision*, 77(1-3):259–289, 2008.

[83] B. Leibe and B. Schiele. Interleaved object categorization and segmentation. In *British Machine Vision Conference*, pages 759–768, 2003.

[84] B. Leibe and B. Schiele. Scale invariant object categorization using a scale-adaptive mean-shift search. In *Deutsche Arbeitsgemeinschaft für Mustererkennung*, volume 3175, pages 145–153, 2004.

[85] B. Leibe, E. Seemann, and B. Schiele. Pedestrian detection in crowded scenes. In *Computer Vision and Pattern Recognition*, pages 878–885, 2005.

[86] R. J. Leigh and D. S. Zee. *The neurology of eye movements*. Contemporary neurology series. Oxford University Press, US, 3 edition, 1999.

[87] A. Levin and Y. Weiss. Learning to combine bottom-up and top-down segmentation. In *European Conference on Computer Vision*, pages 581–594, 2006.

[88] A. Levinshtein, A. Stere, K. N. Kutulakos, D. J. Fleet, S. J. Dickinson, and K. Siddiqi. Turbopixels: Fast superpixels using geometric flows. *Pattern Analysis and Machine Intelligence*, 31(12):2290–2297, 2009.

[89] T. Lindeberg. Automatic scale selection as a pre-processing stage to interpreting real-world data. In *International Conference on Tools with Artificial Intelligence*, pages 490–490, 1996.

[90] Y. Liu, D. Zhang, G. Lu, and W.-Y. Ma. A survey of content-based image retrieval with high-level semantics. *Pattern Recognition*, 40(1):262–282, 2007.

[91] D. G. Lowe. Object recognition from local scale-invariant features. In *International Conference on Computer Vision*, pages 1150–1157, 1999.

[92] D. G. Lowe. Distinctive image features from scale-invariant keypoints. *International Journal of Computer Vision*, 60(2):91–110, 2004.

[93] C. Lu, S. Pizer, S. Joshi, and J. Jeong. Statistical multi-object shape models. *International Journal of Computer Vision*, 75:387–404, 2007.

[94] J. B. MacQueen. Some methods for classification and analysis of multivariate observations. In *Berkeley Symposium on Mathematical Statistics and Probability*, volume 1, pages 281–297, 1967.

[95] T. Malisiewicz and A. A. Efros. Beyond categories: The visual memex model for reasoning about object relationships. In *Neural Information Processing Systems*, 2009.

[96] R. Maree, P. Geurts, and L. Wehenkel. Content-based image retrieval by indexing random subwindows with randomized trees. In *Asian Conference on Computer Vision*, pages 611–620, 2007.

[97] J. Marin, D. Vazquez, D. Geronimo, and A. Lopez. Learning appearance in virtual scenarios for pedestrian detection. In *Computer Vision and Pattern Recognition*, 2010.

[98] D. Marr. *Vision*. Freeman, 1982.

[99] D. Marr and E. Hildreth. Theory of edge detection. In *Proceedings of the Royal Society of London*, volume 207 of *B*, pages 187–217, 1980.

[100] D. Martin, C. Fowlkes, D. Tal, and J. Malik. A database of human segmented natural images and its application to evaluating segmentation algorithms and measuring ecological statistics. In *International Conference on Computer Vision*, pages 416–423, 2001.

[101] J. Matas, O. Chum, M. Urban, and T. Pajdla. Robust wide-baseline stereo from maximally stable extremal regions. *Image and Vision Computing*, 22(10):761 – 767, 2004.

[102] A. McCallum and C. R. Efficiently inducing features of conditional random fields. In *Conference in Uncertainty in Articifical Intelligence*, 2003.

[103] F. Meyer. Topographic distance and watershed lines. *Signal Processing*, 38(1):113–125, 1994.

[104] K. Mikolajczyk and C. Schmid. An affine invariant interest point detector. In *European Conference on Computer Vision*, pages 128–142, 2002.

[105] K. Mikolajczyk and C. Schmid. A performance evaluation of local descriptors. *Pattern Analysis and Machine Intelligence*, 27(10):1615–1630, 2005.

[106] K. Mikolajczyk, C. Schmid, and A. Zisserman. Human detection based on a probabilistic assembly of robust part detectors. In *European Conference on Computer Vision*, volume I, pages 69–81, 2004.

[107] K. Mikolajczyk, T. Tuytelaars, C. Schmid, A. Zisserman, J. Matas, F. Schaffalitzky, T. Kadir, and L. V. Gool. A comparison of affine region detectors. *International Journal of Computer Vision*, 65(1-2):43–72, 2005.

[108] H. Moravec. Towards automatic visual obstacle avoidance. In *International Joint Conference on Artificial Intelligence*, page 584, 1977.

[109] G. Mori, X. Ren, A. Efros, and J. Malik. Recovering human body configurations: combining segmentation and recognition. In *Computer Vision and Pattern Recognition*, volume 2, pages 326–333, 2004.

[110] S. Nowozin, K. Tsuda, T. Uno, T. Kudo, and G. Bakir. Weighted substructure mining for image analysis. *Computer Vision and Pattern Recognition*, pages 1–8, 2007.

[111] R. Okada and S. Soatto. Relevant feature selection for human pose estimation and localization in cluttered images. In *European Conference on Computer Vision*, pages 434–445, 2008.

167

[112] A. Oliva and A. Torralba. Modeling the shape of the scene: A holistic representation of the spatial envelope. *International Journal of Computer Vision*, 42:145–175, 2001.

[113] A. Oliva and A. Torralba. Building the gist of a scene: the role of global image features in recognition. *Progress in Brain Research*, 155:23–36, 2006.

[114] O. F. Olsen and M. Nielsen. Multi-scale gradient magnitude watershed segmentation. In *International Conference on Image Analysis and Processing*, pages 6–13, 1997.

[115] O. C. Ozcanli and B. B. Kimia. Generic object recognition via shock patch fragments. In *British Machine Vision Conference*, pages 1030–1039, 2007.

[116] C. Papageorgiou, T. Evgeniou, and T. Poggio. A trainable pedestrian detection system. In *Intelligent Vehicles*, pages 241–246, 1998.

[117] K. Pearson. On lines and planes of closest fit to systems of points in space. *Philosophical Magazine*, 2(6):559–572, 1901.

[118] S. Pinneli and D. M. Chandler. A Bayesian approach to predicting the perceived interest of objects. *International Conference on Image Processing*, pages 2584–2587, 2008.

[119] S. Pizer, K. Siddiqi, G. Szekely, and S. Zucker. Multiscale medial loci and their properties. *International Journal of Computer Vision*, 55(2-3):155–179, 2003.

[120] N. Plath, M. Toussaint, and S. Nakajima. Multi-class image segmentation using conditional random fields and global classification. In *International Conference on Machine Learning*, pages 817–824, 2009.

[121] L. Pomarjanschi, M. Dorr, C. Rasche, and E. Barth. Safer driving with gaze guidance. In *Proceedings of Bionetics*, 2010. in press.

[122] F. H. Previc and H. Intraub. Vertical biases in scene memory. *Neuropsychologia*, 35(12):1513–1517, 1997.

[123] Bundesamt für Straßenwesen. Verkehrs- und Unfalldaten. http://www.bast.de, 2010.

[124] L. R. Rabiner. A tutorial on hidden markov models and selected applications in speech recognition. In *Readings in speech recognition*, pages 267–296, 1990.

[125] N. Rasiwasia, P. L. Moreno, and N. Vasconcelos. Bridging the gap: Query by semantic example. *IEEE Transactions on Multimedia*, 9(5):923–938, 2007.

[126] N. Rasiwasia, N. Vasconcelos, and P. L. Moreno. Query by semantic example. In *Conference on Image and Video Retrieval*, volume 4071, pages 51–60, 2006.

[127] X. Ren, C. C. Fowlkes, and J. Malik. Learning probabilistic models for contour completion in natural images. *International Journal of Computer Vision*, 77(1-3):47–63, 2008.

[128] X. Ren and J. Malik. Learning a classification model for segmentation. In *International Conference on Computer Vision*, pages 10–17, 2003.

[129] M. Riesenhuber and T. Poggio. Hierarchical models of object recognition in cortex. *Nature Neuroscience*, 2:1019 – 1025, 1999.

[130] E. Rosch, C. B. Mervis, W. D. Gray, D. M. Johnson, and P. B. Braem. Basic objects in natural categories. *Cognitive Psychology*, 8(3):382–439, July 1976.

[131] C. Rother, V. Kolmogorov, and A. Blake. Grabcut: Interactive foreground extraction using iterated graph cuts. *ACM Transactions on Graphics*, 23:309–314, 2004.

[132] Y. Rubner, C. Tomasi, and L. J. Guibas. The earth mover's distance as a metric for image retrieval. *International Journal of Computer Vision*, 40(2):99–121, 2000.

[133] B. C. Russell, A. Torralba, K. P. Murphy, and W. T. Freeman. Labelme: A database and web-based tool for image annotation. *International Journal of Computer Vision*, 77:157–173, 2007.

[134] A. Saxena, S. H. Chung, and A. Y. Ng. 3-d depth reconstruction from a single still image. *International Journal of Computer Vision*, 76:2007, 2007.

[135] F. Schaffalitzky and A. Zisserman. Multi-view matching for unordered image sets, or "how do i organize my holiday snaps?". In *European Conference on Computer Vision*, pages 414–431, 2002.

[136] F. Schaffalitzky and A. Zisserman. Automated location matching in movies. *Computer Vision and Image Understanding*, 92(2):236–264, 2003.

[137] B. Schoelkopf and A. J. Smola. *Learning with Kernels: Support Vector Machines, Regularization, Optimization, and Beyond*. MIT Press, Cambridge, MA, USA, 2001.

[138] T. Serre, L. Wolf, and T. Poggio. Object recognition with features inspired by visual cortex. In *Conference on Computer Vision and Pattern Recognition*, volume 2, pages 994–1000, 2005.

[139] J. Shi and J. Malik. Normalized cuts and image segmentation. *Pattern Analysis and Machine Intelligence*, 22:888–905, 2000.

[140] N. V. Shirahatti and K. Barnard. Evaluating image retrieval. In *Computer Vision and Pattern Recognition*, volume 1, pages 955–961, 2005.

[141] K. Siddiqi, S. Bouix, A. Tannenbaum, and S. Zucker. The hamilton-jacobi skeleton. In *International Conference on Computer Vision*, pages 828–834, 1999.

[142] L. Sigal, S. Bhatia, S. Roth, M. J. Black, and M. Isard. Tracking loose-limbed people. *Computer Vision and Pattern Recognition*, 1:421–428, 2004.

[143] A. W. M. Smeulders, M. Worring, S. Santini, A. Gupta, and R. Jain. Content-based image retrieval at the end of the early years. *Pattern Analysis and Machine Intelligence*, 22(12):1349–1380, 2000.

[144] L. Söderberg. Playboy november 1972. Printed, November 1972.

[145] M. Spain and P. Perona. Measuring and Predicting Object Importance. *International Journal of Computer Vision*, 91(1):59–76, Aug. 2010.

[146] J. Stahl and S. Wang. Edge grouping combining boundary and region information. *Image Processing*, 16:2590–2606, 2007.

[147] H. Steinhaus. Sur la division des corps matriels en parties. *Bull. Acad. Polon. Sci.*, 12:801–804, 1956.

[148] M. Tarr and H. Bülthoff. Image-based object recognition in man, monkey and machine. *Cognition*, 67:1–20, 1998.

[149] W. S. Torgerson. *Theory and Methods of Scaling*. Wiley, 1958.

[150] T. Tuytelaars and L. V. Gool. Content-based image retrieval based on local affinely invariant regions. In *International Conference on Visual Information Systems*, pages 493–500, 1999.

[151] T. Tuytelaars and L. V. Gool. Wide baseline stereo matching based on local, affinely invariant regions. In *British Machine Vision Conference*, pages 412–425, 2000.

[152] V. Uren, Y. Lei, V. Lopez, H. Liu, E. Motta, and M. Giordano. The usability of semantic search tools: a review. *The Knowledge Engineering Review*, 22(04):361–377, 2007.

[153] V. N. Vapnik. *The nature of statistical learning theory*. Springer-Verlag, New York, NY, USA, 1995.

[154] J. Vogel and B. Schiele. On performance characterization and optimization for image retrieval. In *European Conference on Computer Visison*, pages 49–66, 2002.

[155] L. von Ahn, M. Blum, N. J. Hopper, and J. Langford. Captcha: Using hard ai problems for security. In *Eurocrypt*, volume 2656, pages 294–311, 2003.

[156] H. M. Wallach. Conditional random fields: An introduction. Technical Report MS-CIS-04-21, University of Pennsylvania, 2004.

[157] G. Wang, D. Hoiem, and D. Forsyth. Building text features for object image classification. In *Computer Vision and Pattern Recognition*, pages 1367–1374, 2009.

[158] J. Wang, B. Thiesson, Y. Xu, and M. Cohen. Image and video segmentation by anisotropic kernel mean shift. In *European Conference onf Computer Vision*, number 3022 in 2, pages 238–249, 2004.

[159] Y. Wang and S.-C. Zhu. Perceptual scale-space and its applications. *International Journal of Computer Vision*, 80(1):143–165, 2008.

[160] Y. Weiss. Segmentation using eigenvectors: A unifying view. In *International Conference on Computer Vision*, pages 975–982, 1999.

[161] L. Wolf and S. Bileschi. A critical view of context. *International Journal of Computer Vision*, 69(2):251–261, 2006.

[162] C. Xu and J. Prince. Gradient vector flow: A new external force for snakes. In *Computer Vision and Pattern Recognition*, volume 1, pages 66–71, 1997.

[163] C. Xu and J. Prince. Snakes, shapes, and gradient vector flow. *IEEE Transactions on Image Processing*, 7:359–369, 1998.

[164] C. Yang, R. Duraiswami, and L. Davis. Efficient mean-shift tracking via a new similarity measure. In *Computer Vision and Pattern Recognition*, pages 176–183, 2005.

[165] S. Zhu. Embedding gestalt laws in markov random fields. *Pattern Analysis and Machine Intelligence*, 21(11):1170–1187, 1999.

[166] S. C. Zhu and A. L. Yuille. Forms: a flexible object recognition and modeling system. *International Journal of Computer Vision*, 20(3):187–212, 1996.